Kistler

GENDER ADVERTISEMENTS

GENDER ADVERTISEMENTS

Erving Goffman

HARPER COLOPHON BOOKS
Harper & Row, Publishers
New York, Hagerstown, San Francisco, London

First HARPER COLOPHON edition published 1979.

ISBN: 0-06-090633-0

80 81 82 83 10 9 8 7 6 5 4 3

CONTENTS

ACKNOWLEDGEMENTS

Apart from a few changes, this monograph first appeared as vol. 3, no. 2 (Fall 1976) of *Studies in the Anthropology of Visual Communication*, a publication of the Society for the Anthropology of Visual Communication. I am very grateful to its then editor, the late Sol Worth, for support in working out the original edition and for permission to use its plates and glossies. I am also grateful to Elsa Vorwerk, managing editor of the American Anthropological Association, for a great deal of help with the original layout. The slides from which the reproductions were made were themselves done from the originals by John Carey and Lee Ann Draud.

INTRODUCTION
by Vivian Gornick

The contemporary feminist movement, with all its clamor about the meaning of the little details in daily life, has acted as a kind of electric prod to the thought of many social scientists, giving new impetus and direction to their work, the very substance of which is the observation of concrete detail in social life. Because of the feminists the most ordinary verbal exchange between men and women now reverberates with new meaning; the most simple gesture, familiar ritual, taken-for-granted form of address has become a source of new understanding with regard to relations between the sexes and the social forces at work behind those relations. Operating out of "a politics that originates with one's own hurt feelings," the feminists have made vivid what the social scientists have always known: It is in the details of daily exchange that the discrepancy between actual experience and apparent experience is to be found.

Erving Goffman is a brilliant social scientist who has spent his life observing social behavior the way a fine literary critic reads literature. He does not sacrifice the text to theory, he knows one reads out of it rather than into it, he never forgets that both the text and society are alive.

At the same time, Goffman's reading of the text is informed by a piece of systematic thought about social behavior that has been gathering shape and force over a great many years. He knows that the details of social behavior are symptomatic revelations of how a sense of self is established and reinforced, and that that sense of self, in turn, both reflects and cements the social institutions upon which rests a culture's hierarchical structure. Like the really fine teacher he is, Goffman is always working to demonstrate that if one examines the details of social life with a highly conscious eye one learns—deeply—who and what one is in the socially organized world.

In this wonderfully dense and lively monograph Goffman turns his attention, specifically, to the ways in which men and women—mainly women—are pictured in advertisements (those highly manipulated representations of recognizable scenes from "real life"), and speculates richly on what those ads tell us about ourselves; what the interplay is between fashioned image and so-called natural behavior; the degree to which advertisements embody an artificial pose reflecting on perhaps yet another artificial pose—that is, the process by which we come to think of what we call our natural selves.

This question of men and women in advertisements is interesting and important, Goffman says, because "So deeply does the male-female difference inform our ceremonial life that one finds here a very systematic 'opposite number' arrangement," one that allows us to think profitably about the way in which self-definition is guided and externally determined.

For Goffman, social situations are settings for ceremonies whose function is "to affirm social arrangements and announce ultimate doctrine." In the social or public situation the most minute behavior has meaning. Gesture, expression, posture reveal not only how we feel about ourselves but add up, as well, to an entire arrangement—a scene—that embodies cultural values.

Within these scenes, Goffman posits, human behaviors can be seen as "displays." Explaining that in animals a display is an "emotionally motivated behavior [that] becomes formalized, provides a readily readable expression of [the animal's] situation, specifically his intent, [and] this...allows for the negotiation of an efficient response from and to witnesses of the display," Goffman goes on to say that, similarly, in human beings "...an individual's behavior and appearance informs those who witness him...about his social identity, mood, intent. ... [T]hese are displays that establish the terms of the contact...for the dealings that are to ensue between the persons providing the display and the persons perceiving it."

But, Goffman adds—and this "but" is the heart of the matter—"The human use of displays is complicated by the human capacity for reframing behavior.... [D]isplays (in humans) are a symptom, not a portrait.... It is not so much the character of an entity that gets expressed.... [E]xpression in the main is not instinctive but socially learned and socially patterned.... [Individuals] are learning to be objects that have a character, that express this character, and for whom this characterological expressing is only natural. We are socialized to confirm our own hypotheses about our natures...."

Turning then to the specific subject of the work in hand, Goffman observes: "What the human nature of males and females really consists of, then, is a capacity to learn to provide and to read depictions of masculinity and feminity and a willingness to adhere to a schedule for presenting these pictures, and this capacity they have by virtue of being persons, not females or males."

It is around this last, wholly persuasive perception that *Gender Advertisements* is organized. Advertisements depict for us not necessarily how we actually behave as men and women but how we *think* men and women behave. This depiction serves the social purpose of convincing us that this is how men and women *are*, or want to be, or should be, not only in relation to themselves but in relation to each other. They orient men and women to the *idea* of men and women acting in concert with each other in the larger play or scene or arrangement that is our social life. That orientation accomplishes the task a society has of maintaining an essential order, an undisturbed on-goingness, regardless of the actual experience of its participants.

In a crucial passage Goffman argues that in one sense the job of the advertiser and the job of a society are the same: "Both must transform otherwise opaque goings-on into easily readable form." *Otherwise opaque goings-on!* A wonderful phrase that speaks volumes. What exactly are the goings-on that are opaque? They are the murky, muddled efforts of the half-conscious mind, the confused spirit, the unresolved will to comprehend the nature of actual experience rather than described experience, felt emotion rather than cued emotion, perceived truth rather than received wisdom. And the "willingness to adhere to a schedule for presenting these pictures" is the inclination both of individuals and of societies to fall back from the conscious struggle to understand ourselves; to learn about ourselves at a remove; to accept as real an almost wholly assumed self.

Speaking in a sense to this highly significant inclination, Goffman remarks—with his genius for brilliant analogy—that it is not at all unlikely that a family on vacation might take its cues for what "having a good time" is from external sources and might, in fact, contrive to look and act like the idealized family-on-vacation in a Coca-Cola ad. By the same token, it hardly needs stressing, men and women take their cues about "gender behavior" from the image of that behavior that advertising throws back at them, and they contrive to become the "people" in those ads.

Reflecting on the intimate give-and-take between *how* photographed advertisements are made, and *what* they are made out of, Goffman concludes: "In seeing what picture makers can make of situational materials one can begin to see what we ourselves might be engaged in doing."

The pictures that Goffman has chosen and arranged for our perusal in *Gender Advertisements* are, then, a commentary on the complicated matter of "what we ourselves might be engaged in doing." That commentary clearly demonstrates that while advertisements appear to be photographing male and female human beings what they are actually photographing is a depiction of masculinity and femininity that is fitted or matched in such a way as to make it function socially.

Now this perception is not original with Goffman (as Goffman himself would be the first to admit; he is eminently fair about identifying his sources). One of the major points of concentration in the feminist strategy has been the image of women in advertising. Many feminists have paid elaborate attention to the frightening uses to which women have been put in ads either as creatures of embodied sexual usage or as thoroughly mindless domestics thrown into ecstasy by a waxed floor or depression by an unbleached shirt. Moreover, the feminists have also pointed out the social and political purposes served by advertisements reinforcing the notion of men as naturally dominant and women as naturally subordinate.

What *is* original with Goffman is the quality of the insight he brings to bear on male-female images in advertising. Most observation on this subject has been of a blunt and fundamental nature: original spadework, so to speak; digging up the issue. What Goffman does here in *Gender Advertisements*—by virtue of his penetrating eye and his comprehensive context—is to contribute an observation so shrewd and subtle it takes us farther than we have been before. For a reader already familiar with the feminist angle of vision trained on the image of women in ads this, of course, is pure pleasure, an unexpected gift: the gift of renewed stimulation, thought fired once more, mental territory increased.

Instead of looking at clutched detergents and half-naked bodies, Goffman concentrates on hands, eyes, knees; facial expressions, head postures, relative sizes; positioning and placing, head-eye aversion, finger biting and sucking. He also groups the pictures so that the bulk of them illustrate in a single series what we think of as a natural pose or piece of behavior for one of the sexes, and then he has the last two or three pictures in the series show the same pose of behavior with the sexes switched. Between the fineness of detail that receives Goffman's attention and the shock value of the switched-sex pictures we experience that inner surprise that precedes deepened perception.

Under headings like "The Feminine Touch," "Function Ranking," "The Ritualization of Subordination," "Relative Size," and "Licensed Withdrawal," Goffman makes us see such observable phenomena in advertising as the following: 1) overwhelmingly a woman is taller than a man only when the man is her social inferior; 2) a woman's hands are seen just barely touching, holding or caressing—never grasping, manipulating, or shaping; 3) when a photograph of men and women illustrates an instruction of some sort the man is always instructing the woman—even if the men and women are actually children (that is, a male child will be instructing a female child!); 4) when an advertisement requires someone to sit or lie on a bed or a floor that someone is almost always a child or a woman, hardly ever a man; 5) when the head or eye of a man is averted it is only in relation to a social, political, or intellectual superior, but when the eye or head of a woman is averted it is always in relation to *whatever* man is pictured with her; 6) women are repeatedly shown mentally drifting from the scene while in close physical touch with a male, their faces lost and dreamy, "as though his aliveness to the surroundings and his readiness to cope were enough for both of them" 7) concomitantly, women, much more than men, are pictured at the kind of psychological loss or remove from a social situation that leaves one unoriented for action (e.g., something terrible has happened and a woman is shown with her hands over her mouth and her eyes helpless with horror).

These details are absorbing and graphic, underlining as they do a sense of things that presses on the alerted mind, the receptive imagination. They make you know better what you have "known" before; they induce the vigorous nod of the head, the murmured "oh yes," the surprised "I hadn't thought of that!"

But Goffman's major contribution in this book of "depicted femininity" (what *Gender Advertisements* is really about) is the continuous, ever-deepening connection he makes between our image of women and the behavior of children. In a shrewd discussion of the child-parent relation he notes that a child's behavior often indicates that "A loving protector is standing by in the wings, allowing not so much for dependency as a copping out of or relief from, the 'realities,' that is, the necessities and constraints to which adults in social situations are subject." He then adds pointedly: "You will note that there is an obvious price the child must pay for being saved from seriousness."

Being saved from seriousness. Another wonderful phrase that echoes endlessly. In series after series of the photographs shown here Goffman leads us to the repeated usage in advertisements of women posed as children, acting like children, looking like children: utterly devoid of the natural sobriety which one associates with the adult mien. Grown women are seen standing with the head cocked way over to the side parallel to the shoulder, face-front, eyes and mouth: *smiling*; or the head tucked into the shoulder, face-front, eyes looking up from under lowered lids, seductive-gamin style; or hands twisted behind the back; or the toes of one foot standing on the toes of the other in a child's "Aw gosh gee" posture; or arms and legs flying off in all directions like a clown; or hands dug deep into the pockets, the facial expression "wicked" or "merry"; and on every last face that damned "dazzling" smile.

Underscoring these observations of women imaged as children is an extraordinary discussion in words and pictures of the way in which we perceive men and women wearing clothes in advertisements. In this discussion Goffman points out that whatever a man is wearing in an advertisement he wears seriously, whereas whatever a woman is wearing she appears to be trying on, as though the clothes were a costume, not the appropriate covering of a person being seriously presented. If a man in an advertisement is wearing a business suit and carrying a briefcase we believe that he is seriously representing a businessman; if the same man is seen wearing shorts and carrying a racquet we believe, equally, that he is representing the same man playing tennis, that we are looking at different aspects of the same life, the one momentarily discarded for the other. However, when we see a woman wearing formal or informal, business or sports clothes we feel we are watching a model play-acting. We cannot believe in the seriousness of the person meant to be represented by the clothes the model is wearing. We feel we are watching someone at a perpetual costume ball, playing at trying on this and that, not someone whose clothes indicate a person seriously present in the social situation being pictured.

Goffman's observation is powerful. One has only to look at an advertisement showing a woman carrying an attache case, or reading 'The Wall Street Journal', or wearing a white coat in a laboratory setting—the words "For the woman with a mind of her own" scrawled across the ad—and then consult one's own instinctive incredulity, to *know* the truth of what he is pointing out. There comes suddenly to mind the memory of old-time vaudevillians in black-face—powerless people "playing" even more powerless people—and it occurs that these images in advertising of women playing at being serious people are a true mock-up of life: an image reflecting an image reflecting an image; trick mirrors, illusory effects, tracings that resemble an idea of human beings, void of real intent, substantive life....Or perhaps Goffman is saying this *is* real life. That is, this is the reality of the life we are living out.

The most painful and perhaps the most important sentence in *Gender Advertisements* is this: "Although the pictures shown here cannot be taken as representative of gender behavior in real life... one can probably make a significant negative statement about them, namely, that *as pictures* they are not perceived as peculiar and unnatural."

What Erving Goffman shares with contemporary feminists is the felt conviction that beneath the surface of ordinary social behavior innumerable small murders of the mind and spirit take place daily. Inside most people, behind a socially useful image of the self, there is a sentient being suffocating slowly to death in a Kafkaesque atmosphere, taken as "natural," that denies not only the death but the live being as well.

Gender Advertisements is an act of creative documentation. Its aim—like that of a fine novel or a sensitive analysis or a live piece of politics—is to name and re-name and name yet again "the thing itself"; to make us see the unnatural in the natural in order that we may rescue the warm life trapped inside the frozen image.

GENDER DISPLAY

I Take it that the function of ceremony reaches in two directions, the affirmation of basic social arrangements and the presentation of ultimate doctrines about man and the world. Typically these celebrations are performed either by persons acting to one another or acting in concert before a congregation. So "social situations" are involved—defining these simply as physical arenas anywhere within which persons present are in perceptual range of one another, subject to mutual monitoring—the persons themselves being definable solely on this ground as a "gathering."

It is in social situations, then, that materials for celebrative work must be found, materials which can be shaped into a palpable representation of matters not otherwise packaged for the eye and the ear and the moment. And found they are. The divisions and hierarchies of social structure are depicted microecologically, that is, through the use of small-scale spatial metaphors. Mythic historic events are played through in a condensed and idealized version. Apparent junctures or turning points in life are solemnized, as in christenings, graduation exercises, marriage ceremonies, and funerals. Social relationships are addressed by greetings and farewells. Seasonal cycles are given dramatized boundaries. Reunions are held. Annual vacations and, on a lesser scale, outings on weekends and evenings are assayed, bringing immersion in ideal settings. Dinners and parties are given, becoming occasions for the expenditure of resources at a rate that is above one's mundane self. Moments of festivity are attached to the acquisition of new possessions.

In all of these ways, a situated social fuss is made over what might ordinarily be hidden in extended courses of activity and the unformulated experience of their participants; in brief, the individual is given an opportunity to face directly a representation, a somewhat iconic expression, a mock-up of what he is supposed to hold dear, a presentation of the supposed ordering of his existence.

A single, fixed element of a ceremony can be called a "ritual"; the interpersonal kind can be defined as perfunctory, conventionalized acts through which one individual portrays his regard for another to that other.

II If Durkheim leads us to consider one sense of the term ritualization, Darwin, in his *Expression of Emotion in Man and Animals*, leads us, coincidentally, to consider quite another. To paraphrase Julian Huxley (and the ethological position), the basic argument is that under the pressure of natural selection certain emotionally motivated behaviors become formalized—in the sense of becoming simplified, exaggerated, and stereotyped—and loosened from any specific context of releasers, and all this so that, in effect, there will be more efficient signalling, both inter- and intra-specifically.[1] These behaviors are "displays," a species-utilitarian notion that is at the heart of the ethological conception of communication. Instead of having to play out an act, the animal, in effect, provides a readily readable expression of his situation, specifically his intent, this taking the form of a "ritualization" of some portion of the act itself, and this indication (whether promise or threat) presumably allows for the negotiation of an efficient response from, and to, witnesses of the display. (If Darwin leads here, John Dewey, and G. H. Mead are not far behind.)

The ethological concern, then, does not take us back from a ritual performance to the social structure and ultimate beliefs in which the performer and witness are embedded, but forward into the unfolding course of socially situated events. Displays thus provide evidence of the actor's *alignment* in a gathering, the position he seems prepared to take up in what is about to happen in the social situation. Alignments tentatively or indicatively establish the terms of the contact, the mode or style or formula for the dealings that are to ensue among the individuals in the situation. As suggested, ethologists tend to use the term communication here, but that might be loose talk. Displays don't communicate in the narrow sense of the term; they don't enunciate something through a language of symbols openly established and used solely for that purpose. They provide evidence of the actor's alignment in the situation. And displays are important insofar as alignments are.

A version of display for humans would go something like this: Assume all of an individual's behavior and appearance informs those who witness him, minimally telling them something about his social identity, about his mood, intent, and expectations, and about the state of his relation to them. In every culture a distinctive range of this indicative behavior and appearance becomes specialized so as to more routinely and perhaps more effectively perform this informing function, the informing coming to be the controlling role of the performance, although often not avowedly so. One can call these indicative events displays. As suggested, they tentatively establish the terms of the contact, the mode or style or formula for the dealings that are to ensue between the persons providing the display and the persons perceiving it.

Finally, our special concern: If gender be defined as the culturally established correlates of sex (whether in consequence of biology or learning), then gender display refers to conventionalized portrayals of these correlates.

III What can be said about the structure of ritual-like displays?

(1) Displays very often have a dialogic character of a statement-reply kind, with an expression on the part of one individual calling forth an expression on the part of another, the latter expression being understood to be a response to the first.

These statement-response pairs can be classified in an

---

[1] *Philosophical Transactions of the Royal Society of London*, Series B, No. 772, Vol. 251 (Dec. 29, 1966), p. 250.

obvious way. There are symmetrical and asymmetrical pairs: mutual first-naming is a symmetrical pair, first-name/sir is an asymmetrical one. Of asymmetrical pairs, some are dyadically reversible, some not: the greetings between guest and host, asymmetrical in themselves, may be reversed between these two persons on another occasion; first-name/title, on the other hand, ordinarily is not reversible. Of dyadically irreversible pairs of rituals, some pair parts are exclusive, some not: the civilian title a male may extend a female is never extended to him; on the other hand, the "Sir" a man receives from a subordinate in exchange for first-name, he himself is likely to extend to *his* superordinate in exchange for first-name, an illustration of the great chain of corporate being.

Observe that a symmetrical display between two individuals can involve asymmetries according to which of the two initially introduced the usage between them, and which of the two begins his part of the mutual display first on any occasion of use.

And symmetry (or asymmetry) itself can be misleading. One must consider not only how two individuals ritually treat each other, but also how they separately treat, and are treated by, a common third. Thus the point about symmetrical greetings and farewells extended between a male and a close female friend is that he is very likely to extend a *different* set, albeit equally symmetrical, to her husband, and she, similarly, a yet different symmetrical set to his wife. Indeed, so deeply does the male-female difference inform our ceremonial life that one finds here a very systematic "opposite number" arrangement. For every courtesy, symmetrical or asymmetrical, that a woman shows to almost anyone, there will be a parallel one—seen to be the same, yet different—which her brother or husband shows to the same person.

(2) Given that individuals have work to do in social situations, the question arises as to how ritual can accommodate to what is thus otherwise occurring. Two basic patterns seem to appear. First, display seems to be concentrated at beginnings and endings of purposeful undertakings, that is, at junctures, so that, in effect, the activity itself is not interfered with. (Thus the small courtesies sometimes performed in our society by men to women when the latter must undergo what can be defined as a slight change in physical state, as in getting up, sitting down, entering a room or leaving it, beginning to smoke or ceasing to, moving indoors or outdoors, suffering increased temperature or less, and so forth.) Here one might speak of "bracket rituals." Second, some rituals seem designed to be continued as a single note across a strip of otherwise intended activity without displacing that activity itself. (Thus the basic military courtesy of standing at attention throughout the course of an encounter with a superior—in contrast to the salute, this latter clearly a bracket ritual.) One can speak here of a "ritual transfix" or "overlay." Observe that by combining these two locations—brackets and overlays—one has, for any strip of activity, a *schedule* of displays. Although these rituals will tend to be perceived as coloring the whole of the scene, in fact, of course, they only occur selectively in it.

(3) It is plain that if an individual is to give and receive what is considered his ritual due in social situations, then he must—whether by intent or in effect—style himself so that

others present can immediately know the social (and sometimes the personal) identity of he who is to be dealt with; and in turn he must be able to acquire this information about those he thus informs. Some displays seem to be specialized for this identificatory, early-warning function: in the case of gender, hair style, clothing, and tone of voice. (Handwriting similarly serves in the situation-like contacts conducted through the mails; name also so serves, in addition to serving in the management of persons who are present only in reference.) It can be argued that although ritualized behavior in social situations may markedly change over time, especially in connection with politicization, identificatory stylings will be least subject to change.

(4) There is no doubt that displays can be, and are likely to be, multivocal or polysemic, in the sense that more than one piece of social information may be encoded in them. (For example, our terms of address typically record sex of recipient and also properties of the relationship between speaker and spoken to. So, too, in occupational titles ["agentives"]. In the principal European languages, typically a masculine form is the unmarked case; the feminine is managed with a suffix which, in addition, often carries a connotation of incompetence, facetiousness, and inexperience.[2]) Along with this complication goes another. Not only does one find that recognition of different statuses can be encoded in the same display, but also that a hierarchy of considerations may be found which are addressed sequentially. For example, when awards are given out, a male official may first give the medal, diploma, prize, or whatever, and then shake the hand of the recipient, thus shifting from that of an organization's representative bestowing an official sign of regard on a soldier, colleague, fellow citizen, etc., to a man showing regard for another, the shift in action associated with a sharply altered facial expression. This seems nicely confirmed when the recipient is a woman. For then the second display can be a social kiss. When Admiral Elmo R. Zumwalt, then chief of U.S. naval operations, officiated in the ceremony in which Alene Duerk became the first female admiral in the U.S. Navy's history (as director of the Navy Nurse Corps), he added to what was done by kissing her full on the lips.[3] So, too, a female harpist after just completing Ginastera's Harp Concerto, and having just shaken the hand of the conductor (as would a male soloist), is free (as a male is not) to strike an additional note by leaning over and giving the conductor a kiss on the cheek. Similarly, the applause she receives will be her due as a musician, but the flowers that are brought onstage a moment after speak to something that would not be spoken to in a male soloist. And the reverse sequence is possible. I have seen a well-bred father raise his hat on first meeting his daughter after a two-year absence, *then* bend and kiss her. (The hat-raise denoted the relationship between the sexes—presumably "any lady" would have induced it—the kiss, the relation between kin.)

(5) Displays vary quite considerably in the degree of their formalization. Some, like salutes, are specified as to form and occasion of occurrence, and failure to so behave can lead to specific sanctions; others are so much taken for granted that it awaits a student of some kind to explicate what everyone

---

[2] See the thorough treatment of "feminizers" in Conners (1971).
[3] *International Herald Tribune*, June 3-4, 1972.

knows (but not consciously), and failure to perform leads to nothing more than diffuse unease and a search for speakable reasons to be ill-tempered with the offender.

(6) The kind of displays I will be concerned with—gender displays—have a related feature: many appear to be optional.[4] In the case, for example, of male courtesies, often a particular display need not be initiated; if initiated, it need not be accepted, but can be politely declined. Finally, when failure to perform occurs, irony, nudging, and joking complaint, etc., can result—sometimes more as an opportunity for a sally than as a means of social control. Correlated with this basis of looseness is another: for each display there is likely to be a set of functional equivalents wherewith something of the display's effect can be accomplished by alternative niceties. At work, too, is the very process of ritualization. A recipient who declines an incipient gesture of deference has waited until the intending giver has shown his desire to perform it; the more the latter can come to count on this foreclosure of his move, the more his show of intent can itself come to displace the unfolded form.

(7) Ordinarily displays do not in fact provide a representation in the round of a specific social relationship but rather of broad groupings of them. For example, a social kiss may be employed by kin-related persons or cross-sex friends, and the details of the behavior itself may not inform as to which relationship is being celebrated. Similarly, precedence through a door is available to mark organizational rank, but the same indulgence is accorded guests of an establishment, the dependently young, the aged and infirm, indeed, those of unquestionably strong social position and those (by inversion courtesy) of unquestionably weak position. A picture, then, of the relationship between any two persons can hardly be obtained through an examination of the displays they extend each other on any one type of occasion; one would have to assemble these niceties across all the mutually identifying types of contacts that the pair has.

There is a loose gearing, then, between social structures and what goes on in particular occasions of ritual expression. This can further be seen by examining the abstract ordinal format which is commonly generated within social situations. Participants, for example, are often displayed in rankable order with respect to some visible property—looks, height, elevation, closeness to the center, elaborateness of costume, temporal precedence, and so forth—and the comparisons are somehow taken as a reminder of differential social position, the differences in social distance between various positions and the specific character of the positions being lost from view. Thus, the basic forms of deference provide a peculiarly limited version of the social universe, telling us more, perhaps, about the special depictive resources of social situations than about the structures presumably expressed thereby.

(8) People, unlike other animals, can be quite conscious of the displays they employ and are able to perform many of them by design in contexts of their own choosing. Thus instead of merely "displacing" an act (in the sense described

by ethologists), the human actor may wait until he is out of the direct line of sight of a putative recipient, and then engage in a portrayal of attitude to him that is only then safe to perform, the performance done for the benefit of the performer himself or third parties. In turn, the recipient of such a display (or rather the target of it) may actively collaborate, fostering the impression that the act has escaped him even though it hasn't—and sometimes evidentally so. (There is the paradox, then, that what is done for revealment can be partially concealed.) More important, once a display becomes well established in a particular sequence of actions, a section of the sequence can be lifted out of its original context, parenthesized, and used in a quotative way, a postural resource for mimicry, mockery, irony, teasing, and other sportive intents, including, very commonly, the depiction of make-believe scenes in advertisements. Here stylization itself becomes an object of attention, the actor providing a comment on this process in the very act through which he unseriously realizes it. What was a ritual becomes itself ritualized, a transformation of what is already a transformation, a "hyper-ritualization." Thus, the human use of displays is complicated by the human capacity for reframing behavior.

In sum, then, how a relationship is portrayed through ritual can provide an imbalanced, even distorted, view of the relationship itself. When this fact is seen in the light of another, namely, that displays tend to be scheduled accommodatively during an activity so as not to interfere with its execution, it becomes even more clear that the version ritual gives us of social reality is only that—not a picture of the way things are but a passing exhortative guide to perception.

IV Displays are part of what we think of as "expressive behavior," and as such tend to be conveyed and received as if they were somehow natural, deriving, like temperature and pulse, from the way people are and needful, therefore, of no social or historical analysis. But, of course, ritualized expressions are as needful of historical understanding as is the Ford car. Given the expressive practices we employ, one may ask: Where do these displays come from?

If, in particular, there are behavioral styles—codings—that distinguish the way men and women participate in social situations, then the question should be put concerning the origins and sources of these styles. The materials and ingredients can come directly from the resources available in particular social settings, but that still leaves open the question of where the formulating of these ingredients, their *styling*, comes from.

The most prominent account of the origins of our gender displays is, of course, the biological. Gender is assumed to be an extension of our animal natures, and just as animals express their sex, so does man: innate elements are said to account for the behavior in both cases. And indeed, the means by which we initially establish an individual in one of the two sex classes and confirm this location in its later years can be and are used as a means of placement in the management of domestic animals. However, although the signs for establishing placement are expressive of matters biological, why we should think of these matters as essential and central is a cultural matter. More important, where behavioral gender

---

[4] As Zimmerman and West (1977) remind me, the individual has (and seeks) very little option regarding identification of own sex class. Often, however, there will be choice as to which complement of displays is employed to ensure gender placement.

display does draw on animal life, it seems to do so not, or not merely, in a direct evolutionary sense but as a source of imagery—a cultural resource. The animal kingdom—or at least certain select parts of it—provides us (I argue) with mimetic models for gender display, not necessarily phylogenetic ones. Thus, in Western society, the dog has served us as an ultimate model of fawning, of bristling, and (with baring of fangs) of threatening; the horse a model, to be sure, of physical strength, but of little that is interpersonal and interactional.[5]

Once one sees that animal life, and lore concerning that life, provides a cultural source of imagery for gender display, the way is open to examine other sources of display imagery, but now models for mimicry that are closer to home. Of considerable significance, for example, is the complex associated with European court life and the doctrines of the gentleman, especially as these came to be incorporated (and modified) in military etiquette. Although the force of this style is perhaps declining, it was, I think, of very real importance until the second World War, especially in British influenced countries and especially, of course, in dealings between males. For example, the standing-at-attention posture as a means of expressing being on call, the "Sir" response, and even the salute, became part of the deference style far beyond scenes from military life.

For our purposes, there is a source of display much more relevant than animal lore or military tradition, a source closer to home, a source, indeed, right in the home: the parent-child relationship.

V The parent-child complex—taken in its ideal middle-class version—has some very special features when considered as a source of behavioral imagery. First, most persons end up having been children cared for by parents and/or elder sibs, and as parents (or elder sibs) in the reverse position. So both sexes experience both roles—a sex-free resource. (The person playing the role opposite the child is a mother or older sister as much or more than a father or elder brother. Half of those in the child role will be male, and the housewife role, the one we used to think was ideally suitable for females, contains lots of parental elements.) Second, given inheritance and residence patterns, parents are the only authority in our society that can rightly be said to be both temporary and exerted "in the best interests" of those subordinated thereby. To speak here—at least in our Western society—of the child giving something of equivalence in exchange for the rearing that he gets is ludicrous. There is no appreciable quid pro quo. Balance lies elsewhere. What is received in one generation is given in the next. It should be added that this important unselfseeking possibility has been

---

[5] An important work here, of course, is Darwin's *Expression of Emotions in Man and Animals*. In this treatise a direct parallel is drawn, in words and pictures, between a few gestures of a few animals—gestures expressing, for example, dominance, appeasement, fear—and the same expressions as portrayed by actors. This study, recently and rightly resurrected as a classic in ethology (for indeed, it is in this book that displays are first studied in detail in everything but name), is generally taken as an elucidation of our animal natures and the expressions we consequently share with them. Now the book is also functioning as a source in its own right of cultural beliefs concerning the character and origins of alignment expressions.

much neglected by students of society. The established imagery is economic and Hobbesian, turning on the notion of social exchange, and the newer voices have been concerned to show how parental authority can be misguided, oppressive, and ineffective.

Now I want to argue that parent-child dealings carry special value as a means of orienting the student to the significance of social situations as a unit of social organization. For a great deal of what a child is privileged to do and a great deal of what he must suffer his parents doing on his behalf pertains to how adults in our society come to manage themselves in social situations. Surprisingly the key issue becomes this: *What mode of handling ourselves do we employ in social situations as our means of demonstrating respectful orientation to them and of maintaining guardedness within them?*

It might be useful, then, to outline schematically the ideal middle-class parent-child relationship, limiting this to what can occur when a child and parent are present in the same social situation.

It seems to be assumed that the child comes to a social situation with all its "basic" needs satisfied and/or provided for, and that there is no good reason why he himself should be planning and thinking very far into the future. It is as though the child were on holiday.

There is what might be called orientation license. The child is tolerated in his drifting from the situation into aways, fugues, brown studies, and the like. There is license to flood out, as in dissolving into tears, capsizing into laughter, bursting into glee, and the like.

Related to this license is another, namely, the use of patently ineffective means to effect an end, the means expressing a desire to escape, cope, etc., but not possibly achieving its end. One example is the child's hiding in or behind parents, or (in its more attenuated form) behind his own hand, thereby cutting his eyes off from any threat but not the part of him that is threatened. Another is "pummeling," the kind of attack which is a half-serious joke, a use of considerable force but against an adversary that one knows to be impervious to such an effort, so that what starts with an instrumental effort ends up an admittedly defeated gesture. In all of this one has nice examples of ritualization in the classical ethological sense. And an analysis of what it is to act childishly.

Next, protective intercession by parents. High things, intricate things, heavy things, are obtained for the child. Dangerous things—chemical, electrical, mechanical—are kept from him. Breakable things are managed for him. Contacts with the adult world are mediated, providing a buffer between the child and surrounding persons. Adults who are present generally modulate talk that must deal with harsh things of this world: discussion of business, money, and sex is censored; cursing is inhibited; gossip diluted.

There are indulgence priorities: precedence through doors and onto life rafts is given the child; if there are sweets to distribute, he gets them first.

There is the notion of the erasability of offense. Having done something wrong, the child merely cries and otherwise shows contrition, after which he can begin afresh as though the slate had been washed clean. His immediate emotional response to being called to task need only be full enough and it will be taken as final payment for the delict. He can also assume that love will not be discontinued because of what he has done, providing only that he shows how broken up he is because of doing it.

There is an obvious generalization behind all these forms of license and privilege. A loving protector is standing by in the wings, allowing not so much for dependency as a copping out of, or relief from, the "realities," that is, the necessities and constraints to which adults in social situations are subject. In the deepest sense, then, middle-class children are not engaged in adjusting to and adapting to social situations, but in practicing, trying out, or playing at these efforts. Reality for them is deeply forgiving.

Note, if a child is to be able to call upon these various reliefs from realities, then, of course, he must stay within range of a distress cry, or within view—scamper-back distance. And, of course, in all of this, parents are provided scenes in which they can act out their parenthood.

You will note that there is an obvious price that the child must pay for being saved from seriousness.

He is subjected to control by physical fiat and to commands serving as a lively reminder thereof: forced rescues from oncoming traffic and from potential falls; forced care, as when his coat is buttoned and mittens pulled on against his protest. In general, the child's doings are unceremoniously interrupted under warrant of ensuring that they are executed safely.

He is subjected to various forms of nonperson treatment. He is talked past and talked about as though absent. Gestures of affection and attention are performed "directly," without engaging him in verbal interaction through the same acts. Teasing and taunting occur, dealings which start out involving the child as a coparticipant in talk and end up treating him merely as a target of attention.

His inward thoughts, feelings, and recollections are not treated as though he had informational rights in their disclosure. He can be queried on contact about his desires and intent, his aches and pains, his resentments and gratitude, in short, his subjective situation, but he cannot go very far in reciprocating this sympathetic curiosity without being thought intrusive.

Finally, the child's time and territory may be seen as expendable. He may be sent on errands or to fetch something in spite of what he is doing at the time; he may be caused to give up territorial prerogatives because of the needs of adults.

Now note that an important feature of the child's situation in life is that the way his parents interact with him tends to be employed to him by other adults also, extending to nonparental kinsmen, acquainted nonkin, and even to adults with whom he is unacquainted. (It is as though the world were in the military uniform of one army, and all adults were its officers.) Thus a child in patent need provides an unacquainted adult a right and even an obligation to offer help, providing only that no other close adult seems to be in charge.

Given this parent-child complex as a common fund of experience, it seems we draw on it in a fundamental way in adult social gatherings. The invocation through ritualistic expression of this hierarchical complex seems to cast a spate of face-to-face interaction in what is taken as no-contest terms, warmed by a touch of relatedness; in short, benign

control. The superordinate gives something gratis out of supportive identification, and the subordinate responds with an outright display of gratitude, and if not that, then at least an implied submission to the relationship and the definition of the situation it sustains.

> One afternoon an officer was given a call for illegal parking in a commercial area well off his sector. He was fairly new in the district, and it took him awhile to find the address. When he arrived he saw a car parked in an obviously dangerous and illegal manner at the corner of a small street. He took out his ticket book and wrote it up. As he was placing the ticket on the car, a man came out of the store on the corner. He approached and asked whether the officer had come in answer to his call. When the patrolman said that he had, the man replied that the car which had been bothering him had already left and he hoped the patrolman was not going to tag his car. "Hey, I'm sorry, *pal* but it's already written."
> "I expected Officer Reno, he's usually on 6515 car. I'd appreciate it, Officer, if next time you would stop in before you write them up." The patrolman was slightly confused. . . .
> He said politely and frankly, "Mister, how would it look if I went into every store before I wrote up a ticket and asked if it was all right? What would people think I was doing?" The man shrugged his shoulders and smiled. "You're right, son. O.K., forget it. Listen stop in sometime if I can help you with something." He patted the patrolman on the shoulder and returned to his business [Rubinstein 1973:161-162].

Or the subordinate initiates a sign of helplessness and need, and the superordinate responds with a volunteered service. A *Time* magazine story on female police might be cited as an illustration:

> Those [policewomen] who are there already have provided a devastating new weapon to the police crime-fighting arsenal, one that has helped women to get their men for centuries. It worked well for diminutive Patrolwoman Ina Sheperd after she collared a muscular shoplifter in Miami last December and discovered that there were no other cops—or even a telephone—around. Unable to summon help, she burst into tears. "If I don't bring you in, I'll lose my job," she sobbed to her prisoner, who chivalrously accompanied her until a squad car could be found.[6]

It turns out, then, that in our society whenever a male has dealings with a female or a subordinate male (especially a younger one), some mitigation of potential distance, coercion, and hostility is quite likely to be induced by application of the parent-child complex. Which implies that, ritually speaking, females are equivalent to subordinate males and both are equivalent to children. Observe that however distasteful and humiliating lessers may find these gentle prerogatives to be, they must give second thought to openly expressing displeasure, for whosoever extends benign concern is free to quickly change his tack and show the other side of his power.

VI Allow here a brief review. Social situations were defined as arenas of mutual monitoring. It is possible for the student to take social situations very seriously as one natural vantage point from which to view all of social life. After all, it is in social situations that individuals can communicate in the fullest sense of the term, and it is only in them that individuals can physically coerce one another, assault one another, interact sexually, importune one another

---

[6] *Time*, May 1, 1972, p. 60; I leave unconsidered the role of such tales in *Time*'s fashioning of stories.

gesturally, give physical comfort, and so forth. Moreover, it is in social situations that most of the world's work gets done. Understandably, in all societies modes of adaptation are found, including systems of normative constraint, for managing the risks and opportunities specific to social situations.

Our immediate interest in social situations was that it is mainly in such contexts that individuals can use their faces and bodies, as well as small materials at hand to engage in social portraiture. It is here in these small, local places that they can arrange themselves microecologically to depict what is taken as their place in the wider social frame, allowing them, in turn, to celebrate what has been depicted. It is here, in social situations, that the individual can signify what he takes to be his social identity and here indicate his feelings and intent—all of which information the others in the gathering will need in order to manage their own courses of action—which knowledgeability he in turn must count on in carrying out his own designs.

Now it seems to me that any form of socialization which in effect addresses itself to social situations as such, that is, to the resources ordinarily available in any social situation whatsoever, will have a very powerful effect upon social life. In any particular social gathering at any particular moment, the effect of this socialization may be slight—no more consequence, say, than to modify the style in which matters at hand proceed. (After all, whether you light your own cigarette or have it lit for you, you can still get lung cancer. And whether your job termination interview is conducted with delicacy or abruptness, you've still lost your job.) However, routinely the question is that of whose opinion is voiced most frequently and most forcibly, who makes the minor ongoing decisions apparently required for the co-ordination of any joint activity, and whose passing concerns are given the most weight. And however trivial some of these little gains and losses may appear to be, by summing them all up across all the social situations in which they occur, one can see that their total effect is enormous. The expression of subordination and domination through this swarm of situational means is more than a mere tracing or symbol or ritualistic affirmation of the social hierarchy. These expressions considerably constitute the hierarchy; they are the shadow *and* the substance.[7]

And here gender styles qualify. For these behavioral styles can be employed in any social situation, and there receive their small due. When mommies and daddies decide on what to teach their little Johnnys and Marys, they make exactly the right choice; they act in effect with much more sociological sophistication than they ought to have—assuming, of course, that the world as we have known it is what they want to reproduce.

And behavioral style itself? Not very stylish. A means of making assumptions about life palpable in social situations. At the same time, a choreography through which participants present their alignments to situated activities in progress. And the stylings themselves consist of those arrangements of the human form and those elaborations of human action that can be displayed across many social settings, in each case drawing on local resources to tell stories of very wide appeal.

VII

I conclude with a sermon. There is a wide agreement that fishes live in the sea because they cannot breathe on land, and that we live on land because we cannot breathe in the sea. This proximate, everyday account can be spelled out in ever increasing physiological detail, and exceptional cases and circumstances uncovered, but the general answer will ordinarily suffice, namely, an appeal to the nature of the beast, to the givens and conditions of his existence, and a guileless use of the term "because." Note, in this happy bit of folk wisdom—as sound and scientific surely as it needs to be—the land and sea can be taken as there prior to fishes and men, and not—contrary to genesis—put there so that fishes and men, when they arrived, would find a suitable place awaiting them.

This lesson about the men and the fishes contains, I think, the essence of our most common and most basic way of thinking about ourselves: an accounting of what occurs by an appeal to our "natures," an appeal to the very conditions of our being. Note, we can use this formula both for categories of persons and for particular individuals. Just as we account for the fact that a man walks upright by an appeal to his nature, so we can account for why a particular amputee doesn't by an appeal to his particular conditions of being.

It is, of course, hardly possible to imagine a society whose members do not routinely read from what is available to the senses to something larger, distal, or hidden. Survival is unthinkable without it. Correspondingly, there is a very deep belief in our society, as presumably there is in others, that an object produces signs that are informing about it. Objects are thought to structure the environment immediately around themselves; they cast a shadow, heat up the surround, strew indications, leave an imprint; they impress a part picture of themselves, a portrait that is unintended and not dependent on being attended, yet, of course, informing nonetheless to whomsoever is properly placed, trained, and inclined. Presumably this indicating is done in a malleable surround of some kind—a field for indications—the actual perturbations in which is the sign. Presumably one deals here with "natural indexical signs," sometimes having "iconic" features. In any case, this sort of indicating is to be seen neither as physical instrumental action in the fullest sense, nor as communication as such, but something else, a kind of by-production, an overflowing, a tell-tale soiling of the environment wherever the object has been. Although these signs are likely to be distinct from, or only a part of, the object about which they provide information, it is their configuration which counts, and the ultimate source of this, it is felt, is the object itself in some independence of the particular field in which the expression happens to occur. Thus we take sign production to be situationally phrased but not situationally determined.

The natural indexical signs given off by objects we call animal (including, and principally, man) are often called "expressions," but in the sense of that term here implied, our imagery still allows that a material process is involved, not

---

[7] A recent suggestion along this line can be found in the effort to specify in detail the difference between college men and women in regard to sequencing in cross-sexed conversation. See Zimmerman and West (1975), Fishman (1975), and West and Zimmerman (1975). The last discusses some similarities between parent-child and adult male-female conversational practices.

conventional symbolic communication. We tend to believe that these special objects not only give off natural signs, but do so more than do other objects. Indeed, the emotions, in association with various bodily organs through which emotions most markedly appear, are considered veritable engines of expression. As a corollary, we assume that among humans a very wide range of attributes are expressible: intent, feeling, relationship, information state, health, social class, etc. Lore and advice concerning these signs, including how to fake them and how to see behind fakeries, constitute a kind of folk science. All of these beliefs regarding man, taken together, can be referred to as the doctrine of natural expression.

It is generally believed that although signs can be read for what is merely momentarily or incidentally true of the object producing them—as, say, when an elevated temperature indicates a fever—we routinely seek another kind of information also, namely, information about those of an object's properties that are felt to be *perduring, overall,* and *structurally basic,* in short, information about its character or "essential nature." (The same sort of information is sought about classes of objects.) We do so for many reasons, and in so doing presume that objects (and classes of objects) have natures independent of the particular interest that might arouse our concern. Signs viewed in this light, I will call "essential," and the belief that they exist and can be read and that individuals give them off is part of the doctrine of natural expression. Note again, that although some of these attributes, such as passing mood, particular intent, etc., are not themselves taken as characteristic, the *tendency* to possess such states and concerns is seen as an essential attribute, and conveying evidence of internal states in a particular manner can be seen as characteristic. In fact, there seems to be no incidental contingent expression that can't be taken as evidence of an essential attribute; we need only see that to respond in a particular way to particular circumstances is what might be expected in general of persons as such or a certain kind of person or a particular person. Note, any property seen as unique to a particular person is likely also to serve as a means of characterizing him. A corollary is that the absence in him of a particular property seen as common to the class of which he is a member tends to serve similarly.

Here let me restate the notion that one of the most deeply seated traits of man, it is felt, is gender; femininity and masculinity are in a sense the prototypes of essential expression—something that can be conveyed fleetingly in any social situation and yet something that strikes at the most basic characterization of the individual.

But, of course, when one tries to use the notion that human objects give off natural indexical signs and that some of these expressions can inform us about the essential nature of their producer, matters get complicated. The human objects themselves employ the term "expression," and conduct themselves to fit their own conceptions of expressivity; iconicity especially abounds, doing so because it has been made to. Instead of our merely obtaining expressions of the object, the object obligingly gives them to us, conveying them through ritualizations and communicating them through symbols. (But then it can be said that this giving itself has unintended expressive features: for it does

not seem possible for a message to be transmitted without the transmitter and the transmission process blindly leaving traces of themselves on whatever gets transmitted.)

There is, straight off, the obvious fact that an individual can fake an expression for what can be gained thereby; an individual is unlikely to cut off his leg so as to have a nature unsuitable for military service, but he might indeed sacrifice a toe or affect a limp. In which case "because of" becomes "in order to." But that is really a minor matter; there are more serious difficulties. I mention three.

First, it is not so much the character or overall structure of an entity that gets expressed (if such there be), but rather particular, situationally-bound features relevant to the viewer. (Sometimes, for example, no more than that the object is such a one and not another.) The notion of essence, character, structure, is, one might argue, social, since there are likely to be an infinite number of properties of the object that could be selected out as the central ones, and, furthermore, often an infinite number of ways of bounding the object from other ones. Thus, as suggested, an attribute which allows us to distinguish its possessor from those he is seen amongst is likely to enter strongly in our characterization of him.

Second, expression in the main is not instinctive but socially learned and socially patterned; it is a socially defined category which employs a particular expression, and a socially established schedule which determines when these expressions will occur. And this is so even though individuals come to employ expressions in what is sensed to be a spontaneous and unselfconscious way, that is, uncalculated, unfaked, natural. Furthermore, individuals do not merely learn how and when to express themselves, for in learning this they are learning to be the kind of object to which the doctrine of natural expression applies, if fallibly; they are learning to be objects that have a character, that express this character, and for whom this characterological expressing is only natural. We are socialized to confirm our own hypotheses about our natures.

Third, social situations turn out to be more than a convenient field of what we take to be natural expression; these configurations are intrinsically, not merely incidentally, a consequence of what can be generated in social situations.

So our concern as students ought not to be in uncovering real, natural expressions, whatever they might be. One should not appeal to the doctrine of natural expression in an attempt to account for natural expression, for that (as is said) would conclude the analysis before it had begun. These acts and appearances are likely to be anything but natural indexical signs, except insofar as they provide indications of the actor's interest in conducting himself effectively under conditions of being treated in accordance with the doctrine of natural expression. And insofar as natural expressions of gender are—in the sense here employed—natural and expressive, what they naturally express is the capacity and inclination of individuals to portray a version of themselves and their relationships at strategic moments—a working agreement to present each other with, and facilitate the other's presentation of, gestural pictures of the claimed reality of their relationship and the claimed character of their human nature. The competency to produce these portraits, and interpret those produced by others, might be said to be essential to our nature, but this competency may provide a very poor picture of the overall relationship between the sexes. And indeed, I think it does. What the relationship between the sexes objectively is, taken as a whole, is quite another matter, not yet well analyzed.

What the human nature of males and females really consists of, then, is a capacity to learn to provide and to read depictions of masculinity and femininity and a willingness to adhere to a schedule for presenting these pictures, and this capacity they have by virtue of being persons, not females or males. One might just as well say there is no gender identity. There is only a schedule for the portrayal of gender. There is no relationship between the sexes that can so far be characterized in any satisfactory fashion. There is only evidence of the practice between the sexes of choreographing behaviorally a portrait of relationship. And what these portraits most directly tell us about is not gender, or the overall relationship between the sexes, but about the special character and functioning of portraiture.

One can say that female behavioral style "expresses" femininity in the sense of providing an incidental, gratuitous portrait. But Durkheim recommends that such expression is a political ceremony, in this case affirming the place that persons of the female sex-class have in the social structure, in other words, holding them to it. And ethologists recommend that feminine expression is an indication of the alignment a person of the female sex class proposes to take (or accept) in the activity immediately to follow—an alignment which does not merely express subordination but in part constitutes it. The first points out the stabilizing influence of worshipping one's place in the social scheme of things, the second, the substantial consequences of minor allocations. Both these modes of functioning are concealed from us by the doctrine of natural expression; for that doctrine teaches us that expressions occur simply because it is only natural for them to do so—no other reason being required. Moreover, we are led to accept as a portrait of the whole something that actually occurs at scheduled moments only, something that provides (in the case under question) a reflection not of the differential nature of persons in the two sex classes but of their common readiness to subscribe to the conventions of display.

Gender displays, like other rituals, can iconically reflect fundamental features of the social structure; but just as easily, these expressions can counterbalance substantive arrangements and compensate for them. If anything, then, displays are a symptom, not a portrait. For, in fact, whatever the fundamental circumstances of those who happen to be in the same social situation, their behavioral styles can affirm a contrary picture.

Of course, it is apparent that the niceties of gender etiquette provide a solution for various organizational problems found in social situations—such as who is to make minor decisions which seem better lost than unresolved, who is to give way, who to step forward, who is to follow, who to lead, so that turns, stops, and moving about can be coordinated, and beginnings and endings synchronized. (In the same way, at the substantive level, the traditional division of labor between the sexes provides a workable solution to the organization of certain personal services, the ones we call domestic; similarly, sex-biased linguistic practices, such as the use of "he" as the unmarked relative pronoun for "individual"—amply illustrated in this paper—provide a basis for unthinkingly concerted usage upon which the efficiency of language depends.) But just why gender instead of some other attribute is invoked to deal with these organizational problems, and how well adapted gender is for doing so, is an open question.

In sum, gender, in close connection with age-grade, lays down more, perhaps, than class and other social divisions an understanding of what our ultimate nature ought to be and how and where this nature ought to be exhibited. And we acquire a vast corpus of accounts to be used as a source of good, self-sufficient reasons for many of our acts (particularly as these determine the allocation of minor indulgences and deprivations), just as others acquire a sovereign means of accounting for our own behavior. Observe, there is nothing superficial about this accounting. Given our stereotypes of femininity, a particular woman will find that the way has been cleared to fall back on the situation of her entire sex to account to herself for why she should refrain from vying with men in matters mechanical, financial, political, and so forth. Just as a particular man will find that his failure to exert priority over women in these matters reflects on him personally, giving him warrant for insisting on success in these connections. (Correspondingly, he can decline domestic tasks on the general ground of his sex, while identifying any of his wife's disinclination here as an expression of her particular character.) Because these stereotypes begin to be applied by and to the individual from the earliest years, the accounting it affords is rather well implanted.

I have here taken a functionalist view of gender display and have argued that what, if anything, characterizes persons as sex-class members is their competence and willingness to sustain an appropriate schedule of displays; only the content of the displays distinguishes the classes. Although this view can be seen as slighting the biological reality of sex, it should not be taken as belittling the role of these displays in social life. For the facilitation of these enactments runs so deeply into the organization of society as to deny any slighting view of them. Gender expressions are by way of being a mere show; but a considerable amount of the substance of society is enrolled in the staging of it.

Nor should too easy a political lesson be drawn by those sympathetic to social change. The analysis of sexism can start with obviously unjust discriminations against persons of the female sex-class, but analysis as such cannot stop there. Gender stereotypes run in every direction, and almost as much inform what supporters of women's rights approve as what they disapprove. A principal means men in our society have for initiating or terminating an everyday encounter on a sympathetic note is to employ endearing terms of address and verbal expressions of concern that are (upon examination) parental in character and profoundly asymmetrical. Similarly, an important ritual available for displaying affectionate concern, emphasizing junctures in discourse, and marking differential conversational exclusiveness is the laying on of the hand, ordinarily an unreciprocatable gesture of male to female or subordinate male.

In all of this, intimacy certainly brings no corrective. In our society in all classes the tenderest expression of affection involves displays that are politically questionable, the place taken up in them by the female being differentiated from and reciprocal to the place taken up by the male. Cross-sex affectional gestures choreograph protector and protected, embracer and embraced, comforter and comforted, supporter and supported, extender of affection and recipient thereof; and it is defined as only natural that the male encompass and the female be encompassed. And this can only remind us that male domination is a very special kind, a domination that can be carried right into the gentlest, most loving moment without apparently causing strain—indeed, these moments can hardly be conceived of apart from these asymmetries. Whereas other disadvantaged groups can turn from the world to a domestic scene where self-determination and relief from inequality are possible, the disadvantage that persons who are female suffer precludes this; the places identified in our society as ones that can be arranged to suit oneself are nonetheless for women thoroughly organized along disadvantageous lines.

And indeed, reliance on the child-parent complex as a source of display imagery is a means of extending intimate comfortable practices outward from their source to the world, and in the wake of this domestication, this only gentling of the world we seem to have, female subordination follows. *Any* scene, it appears, can be defined as an occasion for the depiction of gender difference, and in any scene a resource can be found for effecting this display.

As for the doctrine of expression, it raises the issue of professional, as well as folk, analysis. To accept various "expressions" of femininity (or masculinity) as indicating something biological or social-structural that lies behind or underneath these signs, something to be glimpsed through them, is perhaps to accept a lay theory of signs. That a multitude of "genderisms" point convergently in the same direction might only tell us how these signs function socially, namely, to support belief that there is an underlying reality to gender. Nothing dictates that should we dig and poke behind these images we can expect to find anything there—except, of course, the inducement to entertain this expectation.

REFERENCES CITED

Conners, Kathleen
1971 Studies in Feminine Agentives in Selected European Languages. Romance Philology 24(4):573-598.
Fishman, Pamela
1975 Interaction: The Work Women Do. Paper presented at the American Sociological Association Meetings, San Francisco, August 25-30.
Huxley, Julian
1966 A Discussion on Ritualization of Behaviour in Animals and Man. Philosophical Transactions of the Royal Society of London, Series B, No. 772, Vol. 251:247-526.
Rubinstein, Jonathan
1973 City Police. New York: Farrar, Straus and Giroux.
West, Candace, and Don H. Zimmerman
1975 Women's Place in Conversation: Reflections on Adult-Child Interaction. Paper presented at the American Sociological Association Meetings, San Francisco, August 25-30.
Zimmerman, Don H., and Candace West
1975 Sex Role, Interruptions and Silences in Conversation. *In* Language and Sex: Differences and Dominance. Barrie Thorne and Nancy Henley, eds. Pp. 105-129. Rowley, MA: Newbury House.
1977 Doing Gender. Paper presented at the American Sociological Association Meetings, Chicago.

PICTURE FRAMES[1]

I Pictures—in the sense of still photographs—can be divided into two classes, private and public.

Private pictures are those designed for display within the intimate social circle of the persons featured in them—pictures taken (with or without recourse to a professional photographer) in order to commemorate occasions, relationships, achievements, and life-turning points, whether of a familial or organizational kind.

The special properties of private pictures as part of our domestic ceremonial life are worth considering, and this can be done best, perhaps, by starting with ceremony and working to pictures.

Ritual and ceremonial involve portraiture, involve making palpable to the senses what might otherwise remain buried and tacit in the structure of social life. The traditional argument is that these enactments function to reaffirm basic social arrangements and ultimate beliefs regarding man and nature.

Ritual and ceremonial are accomplished through doings—through making appearances, taking up microecological positions relative to others, performing gestures—and in the nature of doings are soon, if not quickly, completed or played out. (Duration can vary anywhere from the micro-second taken to administer a smile to the six weeks required for the most obdurate of festivities.) As such, these acts can be distinguished from another class of devices which also help (albeit in a very small way) to maintain us in felt support of our social structure: souvenirs, mementoes, gifts, commemoratives, and other relics. These objects, ofttimes directly a part of what it is they celebrate, just as often poorly portray these celebrated social arrangements. But since objects are involved, not actions, things, not enactments, they can last a long time—in the relevant sense forever.

Consider now the pictorial arts. A feature of drawings, paintings, sculpture, and especially photographs, is that these artifacts allow for a combination of ritual and relic. The rendition of structurally important social arrangements and ultimate beliefs which ceremony fleetingly provides the senses, still photography can further condense, omitting temporal sequence and everything else except static visual arrays. And what is caught is fixed into permanent accessi-bility, becoming something that can be attended anywhere, for any length of time, and at moments of one's own choosing.

Thus it is in modern times—and as the modern contribution to ceremonial life—that whenever there is a wedding, an investiture, a birthday party, a graduation exercise, an extended voyage begun or terminated, a picnic, a shop opening, a vacation, or even a visit, snapshots may well be taken, developed, and the prints kept easy to hand.[2] Something like self-worship can thus be accomplished. The individual is able to catch himself at a moment when—for him—he is in ideal surroundings, in association with socially desirable others, garbed in a self-enhancing way (which for white-collar men may mean the rough and manly wear of fishermen, hunters, wranglers, or machinists), poised for a promising take-off, terminating an important engagement, and with a socially euphoric look on his face. A moment when what is visible about him attests to social matters about which he is proud. A moment, in short, when he is in social bloom, ready, therefore, to accept his appearance as a typification of himself.[3] This moment he can dry-freeze and hang on the walls of his house, his office, his shop, his locker, and his wallet, a reference point to which he can return time and again (and long after he can no longer live the scene) as testimonial, as evidence, as depiction, of what his best social self has been and, by implication, must still be. A modest pact with the devil: the individual can shift the ravages of time from his triumphant appearances to his current ones, the only cost being to have slightly spoiled involvement in these former scenes, these high points, consequent on the postural reframing distractively induced by either the immanent prospect of being snapped or the mechanics of doing the snapping or (with Polaroid) a viewing of the viewing.

II *Public* pictures are those designed to catch a wider audience—an anonymous aggregate of individuals unconnected to one another by social relationship and social interaction, although falling within the same market or the same political jurisdiction, the same outreaches of appeal. Here a photographic print is usually not the final form, only a preliminary step in some type of photo-mechanical reproduction in newspapers, magazines, books, leaflets, or posters.

Public pictures themselves are diverse in function and character. For example, there are commercial pictures

---

[1] I have benefited from harsh criticism and a great number of useful suggestions from Sol Worth; also, in a general way, from Goodman (1968).

[2] During the recent European wars, military personnel of all ranks seemed drawn to photographic portraiture in dress uniform—a commonality of ritual orientation that cut across nations and alliances. Why? To provide a memorial image that might well turn out to be the last one? (But then why not in civvies?) To bolster a social identity newly minted and therefore shaky? To mark the occasion of elevation to one's current military rank, whatever that happened to be? Or is the wearing of a uniform that neatly identifies one's situation in life to all viewers (at a time when one suddenly finds oneself in a situation that can be neatly identified) already a kind of portraiture, whose reproduction then momentarily reestablishes protraiture in its normal role?

[3] A similar argument concerning the content of home movies may be found in Chalfen (1975:95-97).

designed to sell a product for an advertiser.

There are news photos, involving matters held to be of current scientific, social, and political concern.

There are instructional pictures, as found, say, in medical text books, the figures in them intended to be anonymous, serving only (apparently) as illustrations of what can be visited on man. (In fact, many illustrations, including the line drawings in dictionaries, are also typifications, a variable mixture unadmittedly responsive to preconceptions concerning the average, the essential, and the ideal.)

There are human interest pictures, also anonymous, ofttimes candid, in which otherwise unnoteworthy individuals confirm our doctrine of expression by eloquently (and presumably unintendedly) choreographing some response, such as fear, puzzlement, surprise, love, shyness, or some inner state, such as joy, hopelessness, innocence, or how we look and what we do when we think no one is present to observe us. To which must be added scenes that a well-placed camera can compose into some sort of "aesthetic" design or into a conventionally evocative portrait of nature. All of these pictured scenes can hopefully be viewed as ends in themselves, timeless, and arty. (In this domain, observe, the line between private and public can waver.[4] Countless enthusiasts are encouraged by a mass hobby apparatus to invest in serious photographic equipment, acquire professional techniques, and take non-family pictures styled for hanging in a gallery. Although only friends and relatives of the household are likely to view the results, in principle they do so "critically" in their capacity as anonymous members of the wider public. And should a larger stage be offered the amateur, the occasion is likely to be seized as recognition, not avoided as an invasion of privacy.)

Finally, there are personal publicity pictures, ones designed to bring before the public a flattering portrait of some luminary, whether political,[5] religious, military, sporting, theatrical, literary,[6] or—where a class elite still functions and is publicized—social.

Involved here are actual or putative leadership and symbolization of some structure or hierarchy or value presentable as central to society. Note, the publicity function extends far beyond personal publicity shots, seeping into almost every kind of picture. Commercial pictures often link a product to a celebrity, selling them both. The pictorial record made of important public ceremonies necessarily gives personal publicity to those who officiate. News events are very often presented through the words and presence of political leaders, a write-up of the first accompanied by a picture of the second. Human interest shots have more interest if they involve famous subjects. Even the celebrity's personal-life rituals can be publicized as a means of affirming in everyone's life what is being affirmed in his own, so that whatever his particular domain, he will tend to become a public performer of private ceremonies and have extra reason on such occasions for taking pictures and ensuring that they are good ones—a mutual contamination of public and private which comes to a head in fan magazines. In the limiting case of a social elite, mere attendance at a particular social function or mere visiting of a particular place can qualify as newsworthy, these performers being empowered to transform social participation from routine into ritual. A reminder that every undertaking has a sacred element and can be done in circumstances which realize its hierarchical potential. Here, may I add, the British Royal Family is the modern creative force, leading the civilized world in know-how for the mass production of personal publicity.

Celebrities not only link their own private lives to the public domain, but also can link the lives of private persons to it. For persons in the public eye representing something of value and concern to many—persons possessing regional or national renown—seem to acquire as one of their powers the capacity to be a contagious high point. Politicians, sports stars, entertainers, and other notables qualify. In contrast to pictures of Jesus, Lenin, and the British Royal Family, those of ordinary celebrities are not always likely to carry enough ritual impact to warrant a place on the mantel; nonetheless, celebrities need but pose for a picture in the company of a member of their public to manufacture a memento for him, one that speaks to his ideal attributes, a sort of elevation by photographically attested association. Note that a personal inscription can function as a weak substitute for joint appearance.[7] (In exchange for their endorsement, then, celebrities acquire a small billboard, rent free.) Thus in bars, restaurants, drycleaning establishments, and offices, these trophies jostle with family pictures, the latter being trophies, too, for they attest to the domestic property (and domestic piety) of the establishment's proprietor, which property, incidentally, has also been photographed in ideal circumstances.

In all of this, note, photographic portraiture represents a rather significant social invention, for, even apart from its role in domestic ritual, it has come to provide a low and very little guarded point in the barrier that both protects and restrains persons of private life from passing over into public recognition.

III To consider photographs—private and public—it is necessary, apparently, to consider the question of perception and reality, and it is necessary to control

---

[4] For this and other suggestions, I am grateful to Dorothea Hurvich.

[5] A deft discussion of political portraits is Roland Barthes' "Photography and Electoral Appeal" (1972:91-93).

[6] For male novelists pictured on the back of their dust covers, this means (currently) rough, open shirts, tousled hair, youthful, virile appearance, and often a brooding look, this last bespeaking the deep thoughts that are proper to the innards of the species. Male poets may feel obliged to appear even more feeling. Nonfiction writers also present pictures of themselves as part of the merchandising of their product, but their posing suggests more the steady march of thought than the psychic cost of so directly addressing the human condition. Interestingly, even those who publish slashing analyses of advertising find reason to allow their pictures to appear on the jacket in a posture calculated to confirm that qualities of the book are to be seen in qualities of the appearance of the writer, thus promoting a folk theory of expression along with their books and themselves.

[7] American presidents have the distinction (one of their few) of having circulated inscribed pictures in their pre-election capacity, and after election circulating ones that qualify as hangable without an inscription.

somehow the systematic ambiguities that characterize our everday talk about pictures.

(1) Pictures comprise the class of two-dimensional images that have been processed into fixed form, the chief examples being drawings, paintings, photographs, and, of course, letterpress reproductions of them all. (What Narcissus saw was a reflection, not a photograph.) A "real" or "actual" photograph consists of a piece of stiff, emulsified paper containing marks and shadings on one side, a text providing us with an image that has been processed photographically, not some other way. (Obviously, a photograph does not embody objects that it pictures—as Sol Worth remarks, a picture of fire is not hot—although some might want to say that the exposed surface does embody a perspectival transformation of some of the relationships within the scene upon which the camera focused.) By this definition it follows that a photograph that has been "touched up," miscaptioned, or even doctored is still a real one. The realness of a photograph would only figure when, say, there was a concern to prevent it from getting crumpled, soiled or torn, or to control the effect of the texture of a paper stock upon depth perception, or to discover that what appeared to be a photograph was indeed a cleverly disguised realistic painting. (What is only something else and not really a photograph involves a slightly different, and certainly lesser, issue than that of what is not really something else but only a photograph. For there are lots of flat, papery things that a photograph can replicate—whether or not with intent to deceive—dollar bills, water colors, and cardiograms being examples; indeed, with experimental controls a photograph pasted into a window can be mistaken for a three dimensional real scene.[8])

Consideration of what is a "real" picture leads to a consideration of what is the "same" picture, and thus to a version of the type-token issue. We speak of the "same" or "identical" picture when referring to two quite different possibilities: two like prints from the self-same negative, and two meetings-up with the self-same print. I don't think this particular ambiguity causes trouble; in any case, unlike the situation with coins, here terminology is ready to hand any time we need to specify.

I believe that the significant question, and one that everyday use and terminology does obscure, is not what a photograph is, or what would count as the same photograph, but what a particular photograph is of—a concern, incidentally, that allows one to treat a photograph and its printing press reproduction as the same.

Somehow we learn to decode small, flat tracings for large, three dimensional scenes in a manner somewhat corresponding to the way we have learned to interpret our visual images of real objects. (Because a photograph has nearly perfect geometric perspective—saving one taken, for example, with a distorting wide-angle lens—it is very like the image projected on the retina of one eye, were the retina to be blocked from its usual scanning; but retinal images themselves are systematically modified by constancy scaling based on additional depth cues drawn in part from stereoscopic and parallax-motion effects which photography must do without.)[9] Here the point is not that our use of our eyes and our pictures has had to be learned, or that this learning draws deeply and fallibly on past experience with the world in all sensory modalities (allowing us to make effective use of small cues and good hypotheses as to which of a set of possible states is to be judged the actual one), but that it *does* get learned (in our society), rendering the eyeing of live scenes, and of pictures of scenes, efficacious and more or less equivalent. And note, this deciphering competency that we acquire with respect to live scenes, and pictures of scenes, does not make us acute about just any set of perceptual details, but rather those which allow us to make conventionally important discriminations; for it is about these matters that are of general social relevance that we will have bothered to accumulate experience.[10] Perhaps, then, the primary difference between an interpretation of a live view and an interpretation of a picture of it is that live viewing ordinarily assures that what is seen is as it appears now, whereas a picture, at best, guarantees that it was once so.

In sum, one can say that, as a result of acquired interpretive competence, things (or rather aspects of things) in effect are as they seem to be seen, and as they seem to be pictured, notwithstanding the fact that the actual image on the retina and on the photographic paper is a somewhat different matter. And one should be able to say that a photograph in effect can provide us with an objective, veridical version—an "actual picture of" socially important aspects of what is in fact out there.

However, these conclusions drawn from the psychology of perception fail to tell us why there should be so much doubt and concern among students as to what in fact photographs do represent. The frame-theoretical issue of the various

---

[8] It is worth noting that art historians who compare various forms of representation—etchings, woodcuts, drawings, paintings, photographs—and use illustrations in their books to explicate the differences, tend to treat the ground of their own operation, letterpress graphics, as something to be taken for granted, something without constraining characteristics of its own, in this following the lay framing practice of treating the medium in which one is oneself working as limitless and featureless.

[9] A close issue here. Apart from the question of permanency, a camera can take an instantaneous picture that contains vastly more detail, shading, and breadth than the eye can capture in the same length of time, the eye being restricted apparently to flitting about taking spot checks which the brain then edits and composes accordingly. However, before the camera's pictures (once developed and printed) can be of any final use, an eye must view it, and *that*

viewing will suffer all the limits of the eye compared to the camera plus an extra set, namely, the limitation of having to start with a photograph, not the real thing.

[10] The framework of experience required in order to interpret some photographs (such as those taken of missile sites, elementary particle pathways, minor meteors) may be so restricted that a lay person might not even be able to see what he is seeing when it is pointed out. However, valid perception is not a question of votes but of competence, W. I. Thomas notwithstanding. And that is not to say that viewers somehow read beyond the "simple" physical images that are "given" them; for a physicalistic, "objective," "literal" description is itself, of course, interpretive, having to be learned, too—a fact quite independent of how common this learning is. There are no naked facts, merely various types of inferential elaboration, but *that* is not to say that inferences, common or otherwise, are necessarily arbitrary.

senses in which pictures are said to be true, real, valid, candid, realistic, expressive, or, contrariwise, false, faked, posed, unfaithful, doctored, guyed, still remains open, and social, not psychological, answers must be sought. The easy sense of the man in the street that the meaning of pictures is clear enough comes from an easy willingness to avoid thinking about the meanings of meaning.

(2) It is clear that an artist can execute a drawing or painting from memory and imagination, processsing an image of, say, a person who is no more or even never was. One might say that the result was a picture of a *subject* (or "figure"), not meaning to imply by this "of" that the subject is now, or ever was, real. Subjects belong to very human realms of being but not always to the current, real world. A subject, note, may be a building or a landscape or a stag at bay or the crossing of the Delaware; it can also be a person, the chief concern here. (French in this regard is clearer than English: a special reference for the word *personnage* designates a member of the fictional realm, the term *personne* being reserved for designating a member of ours.)

Now it happens that when something that is not present to him is to be the subject of a painter's work, he may steady his task of rendition by employing a stand-in, mock-up, or substitute—things of this world that are materially to hand and can serve as guides during phases of the canvas processing. Thus, for an historical figure, he may use a living person there in the flesh; for a mythical beast with unnatural appendages, a real beast with natural ones. A material guide is often called a model, especially when a person or animal is involved, and will be called that here, although other (and confusingly relevant) meanings can also be given to that term (Goffman 1974, esp. 41). Note, incidentally, a parallel distinction in the theater, where it is fully understood that a character or protagonist belongs to a make-believe realm of being that is dramatized, and the actor who takes a part and stages its character belongs to another, namely, everyday reality. Indeed, from the theater comes the term "prop" to remind us that some artifacts have, as it were, no life of their own, taking their identifying title from the fact that their crude similarity to certain objects in the real world (along with their cheapness and maneuverability) allows them to be used in plays as if they were these objects, this role in dramaturgy being their only one.

If one allows that a painter may use a material object as a guide (whether model, prop, or whatever) to help him in his rendering, and if this guiding function is taken as central to one's conception of such objects, then one might extend the category to include objects which the artist uses not only as a guide but also as a subject. After all, to sit for a portrait is to serve as a subject *and* as its model, and so one is forced to say that a stand-in can be the real thing.[11]

Unlike what is required in drawing, painting, or fiction, but like the theater, a photograph *requires* material guides—"models" in the cases that interest us. The play of light and shadow upon something out there in the real world is necessary, and furthermore, is necessary at the moment the picture is taken.

Observe that just as a photograph can be said to be *of* its subject, this being our first sense of "of," so it can be said to be *of* its model, this being our second sense of "of." The convenience of using one word here instead of two, is, I believe, a disaster for analysis, for although biblical paintings and the theatrical stage provide no problem in the distinction between subject and model (or character and actor), photography deeply confounds the matter in several ways—now merging subject and model, now concealing a difference, now taking a difference for granted, and in general causing us to think we are concerned with one problem when we really are concerned about another.

IV (1) A "caught" or "candid" photograph may be defined as featuring models that have not been arrayed to serve as such, that is, to serve as something to photograph on this occasion. Such pictures show objects and events as they are in regard to some matters other than photography. For human models this means ordinarily that they are unaware that a camera is where it is, or that they are so deeply caught up in other vital matters that they either give no weight to the fact that they are being photographed or modify whatever they are doing only to the extent required for a disjunctive monitoring shift in response to the sudden appearance of a camera.[12] (All models can be angled, if not manipulated, for photographic effect; only human ones can do this on their own behalf.) Caught pictures can provide valid documents or records, allowing the viewer to make relatively reliable inferences as to what had led up to the activity represented and what was likely to have

---

[11] Matters can get a little complicated here. A movie actor may be given a stand-in so that in staging a character he himself will not have to engage in tedious or dangerous activity. Clearly (and simply): a model for a model. Novelists, with no intent to engage in covert biography, sometimes pattern a fictional character upon a real person in their social circle, subject and model here being quite distinct, there being an obligation to blur the copy and make a secret of the identity of the model. Biography, on the other hand, allows and requires that the subject and model be one. In biographical plays, then, the character onstage becomes a refraction both of the actor who is taking the part and of the person who was the inspiration for the part. It is a tart experience (or a sad experience), but not necessarily a confusing one, that is produced when the inspiration for a character serves also as the actor of the part, as when the famous gunfighters of the West ended their years by "going on the road" with enactments of themselves. The tricky case is the *roman à clef*, where a connection between subject and model is formally denied (as prefatory admonitions regarding the coincidence of resemblance attest) but

guessing at the identity of the model is encouraged (or at least thought to be), along with the belief that the copying is close.

[12] In fact, matters are a little more complicated. Of the infinite number of scenes photographers might catch, they manage to (and bother to) catch only a small number, and these tend to be ones whose content make evident that the pictures could only have been caught. So a caught picture turns out to be a patently caught one. Also note that whereas the term "caught" seems to be preferentially applied to a scene upon which a camera would have been unlikely, the term "candid" seems to be preferentially used in reference to scenes wherein the participants would ordinarily have been unwilling to continue on with what they had been doing had they but known that a camera was in action. Understandably, some candid pictures present models breaking frame, not only turning precipitously to monitor the camera's intrusion, but also simultaneously attempting to obscure the appearance they had been giving. What is candid about such pictures turns out to be covering behavior, not what the behavior covers.

followed, in the same way, if to a lesser extent, as can an actual viewer of a live scene infer what is going on at the moment of viewing. It is in this way that caught pictures can be used as strong evidence concerning the existence of a state of affairs or of the occurrence of an event. Thus, a pictured individual who can be "personally identified," that is, a subject that provides us with effective evidence of the biographical identification of its model, can serve to demonstrate that its model had been in a certain place doing a certain thing and in association with certain others, which demonstration courts of law may be induced to accept. For example, insurance claims for injuries have been defeated by photographs secretly taken of the claimant while he was engaged in demanding performances, such as bowling, climbing ladders, and the like. Denial of "knowing" someone has similarly been defeated by pictures of the claimant chatting with the person he claims not to know. Bank robbers have faced similar problems due to security photography. In fact, on occasion in courts, claims as to what occurred may find better support through photographs than through direct testimony. Drawings, however realistic, are not used in this particular way, although they can be employed in identificatory police work.[13]

(2) Caught photographs are to be contrasted to another class, whose members share the property that inferences as to what was going on in the scene *cannot* be correctly made from what is pictured.

First, there are photographs (often caught ones) which have been covertly "doctored" or "faked," as when a picture of someone's face is superimposed on a picture of someone else's body, and the whole passed off as evidence that the owner of the face was present in the scene depicted. Or a seriously misleading caption is employed encouraging a false attribution of model to subject.

Second are the kind of pictures that can be said to be arranged, rigged, or set up, implying that models and scenic materials, real enough in their own right, were brought together and choreographed to induce radically wrong inferences as to "who" had been present and/or what had been going on. The result is a picture of a covertly contrived scene; the *picture* is an actual one, but it is not *actually of* the scene it portrays. The classic case here is the collusively arranged infidelity picture, once so popular in British divorce proceedings, providing perfectly valid evidence that a particular man had been in a particular room with a particular woman not his wife, the misleading restricted to their doings and her professional identity. The wrong impression the court is induced to receive (or rather gives the appearance of receiving) is much like the one that the hotel clerk could have obtained of the actual doings, although he might get to see the picture taking as well as the scene the picture taker took. Observe that a doctored picture, whether intended to mislead or not, requires no cooperation from the models, the fabrication being done after, not before, picture taking; rigged pictures, on the other hand, ordinarily require collaborative posing before the picture is snapped, although admittedly if models are caught at the right moment from the right angle, they can find that they have unintentionally produced a picture that is rigged in effect,[14] as they can if they know they are about to be photographed but the photographer does not know they know. Observe, too, that although eyes and cameras can be similarly fooled, it is

---

[13] In his *Art and Illusion*, E. H. Gombrich presents the interesting argument that a picture cannot be true or false in itself, these possibilities being reserved for the caption or label:

Logicians tell us—and they are not people to be easily gainsaid—that the terms "true" and "false" can only be applied to statements, propositions. And whatever may be the usage of critical parlance, a picture is never a statement in that sense of the term. It can no more be true or false than a statement can be blue or green. Much confusion has been caused in aesthetics by disregarding this simple fact. It is an understandable confusion because in our culture pictures are usually labeled, and labels, or captions, can be understood as abbreviated statements. When it is said "the camera cannot lie," this confusion is apparent. Propaganda in wartime often made use of photographs falsely labeled to accuse or exculpate one of the warring parties. Even in scientific illustrations it is the caption which determines the truth of the picture. In a *cause célèbre* of the last century, the embryo of a pig, labeled as a human embryo to prove a theory of evolution, brought about the downfall of a great reputation. Without much reflection, we can all expand into statements the laconic captions we find in museums and books. When we read the name "Ludwig Richter" under a landscape painting, we know we are thus informed that he painted it and can begin arguing whether this information is true or false. When we read "Tivoli," we infer the picture is to be taken as a view of that spot, and we can again agree or disagree with the label. How and when we agree, in such a case, will largely depend on what we want to know about the object represented. The Bayeux tapestry, for instance, tells us there was a battle of Hastings. It does not tell us what Hastings "looked like." [1961:67-68].

In sum, a caption frames a picture, telling us what aspect of it is to be attended and in what light this aspect of matters is to be seen—e.g., the way things once were, the way they might be in the future, the dream of the artist, a tribute to the style of some period, and so forth. But, of course, this approach entirely begs the question. In a great number of contexts an uncaptioned photograph *is* understood to present a claim regarding the properties and character of the model, courts of law only being the most obvious. (The very fact that effort is made to doctor pictures presupposes that ordinarily pictures imply an avowal about reality and that this avowal is ordinarily valid; the same assumption is not made of other modes of representation, and understandably so.) Any object, not merely a picture, is subject to covert simulation and various forms of overt reconstitutings. These transformations nonetheless remain just that, transformations of an original. But granted that the interpretation a picture is given, that is, the sense in which it is taken, derives from the context of use, one must see that the caption, when there is one, is but one part of this context. A caption, then, can be true or false only if *its* context carries another caption, albeit a tacit one: "The statements made here are meant to be taken as avowals of what is." And the reading a caption can cause us to make of a picture, other elements of context can cause us to make of the caption. (The caption "fantasy" can tell us how to read a picture in an art book, but what does it tell us about a picture in the National Lampoon?) A statement of fact, laconic or expanded, can be presented as a quotation, an example of literary style, a display of print format, etc., being no less vulnerable to special readings than are pictures. In any case, a photograph that is falsely captioned (whether to deceive or for openly playful purposes) can still present a perfectly valid representation of its model, the only problem being that the model can't be correctly identified from the caption. May I add that although obviously the angle, light, timing, camera distance, lens, film development, printing, and the photographer's intent can very significantly influence what a picture reproduces, in every case the model must introduce a pattern of constraints as well.

[14] For this, and for other suggestions incorporated without acknowledgment, I am grateful to Richard Chalfen.

usually far easier to hoodwink the viewer of a picture than the viewer of a live scene, for reasons quite apart from, say, the consequence of insufficient depth cues. For the still photographer's practice of holding his camera to a small field and (necessarily) to a single angle can, in the shooting of a rigged scene, protect his illusion from anything disconfirming that might lie just beyond the posing; and what has been posed need only be held long enough to snap it. A live viewer could hardly be restricted this way, and unless he wore blinders and kept his head in a vice, would have to be faced with fakery that is considerably more extensive if it is to be effective—although admittedly he is not often in a position to pore over what he sees for flaws, whereas the viewer of a picture usually is.

(3) Pictures that are covertly doctored or covertly rigged display scenes that can't be read in the same way that uncontrived ones routinely can, as a swarm of warrants for drawing sound conclusions as to who had been present and what had been going on there. Such covertly faked pictures—"fabrications"—are to be distinguished from ones that are also concocted, but this time admittedly, whether by arranging what is photographed or doctoring a photograph already taken.[15] Openly contrived scenes provide a "keying" of photographic evidence as to who was present and what had been going on.[16] The central example here is what might be called "commercial realism," the standard transformation employed in contemporary ads, in which the scene is conceivable in all detail as one that could in theory have occurred as pictured, providing us with a simulated slice of life; but although the advertiser does not seem intent on passing the picture off as a caught one, the understanding seems to be that we will not press him too far to account for just what sort of reality the scene has. (The term "realistic," like the term "sincerity" when applied to a stage actor, is self-contradictory, meaning something that is praiseworthy by virtue of being like something else, although not that something else.) Commercial realism is to be sharply distinguished from scenes posed with unlikely professionals and apparently intended to be wrongly seen as caught, and from scenes that *are* caught ones but now embedded in an advertisement.[17] Observe that commercial realism provides

[15] Currently newspapers and magazines exercise very wide liberty in presenting openly doctored pictures featuring bits of anatomy of celebrities, especially political ones, the portraits completed by line drawings, cartoons, other photographs, and the like. Precisely in what frame readers interpret such pictures is not clear, since what can be legally defended as an evident fantasy may not be so treated by some viewers.

[16] A fuller treatment of "keying" and "fabrication" is presented in Goffman (1974, esp. ch. 3, 4).

[17] There are deviations from commercial realism that are more subtle. Thus, one finds that a picture in an annual company report displaying the company's restaurant equipment with the aid of two secretaries posing as persons dining out and another as a waitress can convey not so much that there is a difference between subject and model, but that these particular models are not making every effort to conceal that they are unprofessional ones, thereby posing as models posing as participants in a restaurant scene. A comparable frame complexity is found in the use of simulated home movies as part of the scenario of a commercial one, or the use in radio commercials of "interviews" with carefully selected ordinary consumers, "citizens," who have been rehearsed into displaying the restarts, filled pauses, and little floodings that presumably distinguish the efforts of real interviewees from the responses performed by studio actors.

especially nice examples of the subject-model issue. Asked what is in a particular ad, we might say, "A family fishing." What makes us think the four subjects in the picture are in a family relationship to one another is exactly what might make us infer such a relationship with respect to strangers in real life. So, too, on seeing images of fishing lines in the water. Asked whether we think the four persons who modeled for the picture are *really* a family or if there are hooks on the lines, the answer could well be, "Probably not, but what does it matter?" The point about an ad is what its composer meant us to infer as to what is going on in the make-believe pictured scene, not what had actually been going on in the real doings that were pictured. The issue is subject, not model.

It is thus that the constraints on picture scene production can be properly sorted. An ad featuring a nude woman subject raises questions about the modesty of the model, especially if she is a well-known one; an ad featuring nuns clustered in front of a station wagon in honor of GM's tilt-wheel steering can (and did) raise questions about the desecration of subjects—the models in this case being well covered by unaccustomed habit (see Livingston 1976).

Advertisements that employ commercial realism or some other variety of overtly concocted scene can be aptly compared to what the stage presents. In both cases the viewer is to engage knowingly in a kind of make-believe, treating the depicted world as if it were real-like but of course not actually real. The differences are interesting. One is that although we undoubtedly can involve ourselves more deeply in staged make-believe than in advertisements, it is probably the case that viewers more frequently reify, that is, "downkey," ads than plays; for we can always fall into thinking that an ad is like a news shot or a private portrait, its model rightly to be identified with its subject. (In any case, the imputation of realness to what a picture is of is unlikely to require our immediate intercession, the presented events having already transpired; on the other hand, when Othello attacks Desdemona, something will have to be done immediately by the audience if they have misframed him as endangering a real life.) Another difference: It is routine in play production that we know the personal identity of the models, at least the lead ones, and that our pleasure in the show derives in part from watching favorite actors at work, whatever the part they are currently at work in. In the case of ads, with very rare exception, the personal identity of the models is unknown to us, and we do not seek out this knowledge. Product testimony by celebrities, or by specially selected citizens whose actual names and addresses are provided, is quite another matter and is by way of being a fraud—a fabrication, not a keying. An interesting marginal case is the *photoroman*, popular on the continent, in which personally identified models—indeed "stars" of the cinematic world—perform for a series of stills in the manner of a comic book, projecting themselves in fictional parts much as they might on the screen, and as on the screen relying on their "own" identities as a source of drawing power (see Van Dormael 1974).

V Starting with caught scenes, the description has been complicated by adding ones that were fabricated and keyed. Now it is essential to go on to see that all these pictures share one important feature, namely, they are all *scenes*, that is, representations, whether candid, faked, or frankly simulated, of "events" happening. Narrative-like action is to be read from what is seen, a before and after are to be inferred, and this location in the ongoing stream of activity provides the context as much as do the models and props *per se*. All such pictures are to be distinguished from another class, namely, portraits, these being pictures—fabricated, keyed, or actually of—where action is absent or incidental, and it cannot quite be said that a scene is in progress. A subject is featured more than a stream of events.

(1) Consider first the matter of the personal portrait format itself. This format was there before the camera came in, has dominated private pictures, and is only now giving way: the model sits or stands in his finery, holds an absent, half-smiling expression on his face in the direction he is instructed to—a constraint only familiar from the military parade ground—and renders himself up to the judgment of eternity, the assumption rightly being that in many ways the model and the subject are one, a case of posing as oneself. No doubt this postural formula reflected the exposure needs of early film and the style (and requirements) established in painted portraiture—providing us a central case of pictures representing other pictures; in any case, no prototype is to be found in the responses individuals, at least sighted ones, have to any other circumstance in the workaday world.[18] (Certainly responses of every kind can be affected and held by brute force for lengthy periods, but these responses are presented as though in reaction *to* something other than picture taking.) When this portrait format is extended to commercial shots featuring a subject and a product, the unseeing expression often gives way to one that is not alien to natural life, merely crudely simulated: a frozen, summoning look, as though the subject were making eye contact, sometimes collusively, with someone there in the flesh behind the shutter, or with a wider group out there in camera land. Also found is an expression of defense against intrusion, a subtle means of encouraging the viewer to feel he is an actual participant in the depicted scene. So, too, subjects, especially female ones, may be shown returning our apparently intrusive look with one that passively submits to our gaze. More subtle still, the subject can give the appearance of turning away from a second figure in the picture sometimes to steal a look at a third figure, in any case allowing us to catch the maneuver from a disclosive angle so that we find ourselves more privy to this disloyalty of attention than is the subject who has lost it. The simulation

of viewer-responsive facial expression by subjects somewhat changes a portrait into a scene and is, of course, a standard feature of Western painting.[19] And note the parallel to a phenomenon peculiar to the legitimate stage called "direct address."

(2) Early private photographic portraits employed canvas backdrops featuring sylvan or hellenic scenes (deemed proper in their three dimensional form to the gentry), thus taking open advantage of the principle that the camera, somewhat like the theatrical stage, drops from the world everything between the figures or objects in central focus and what lies in front, and at the same time tends to reduce what remains of the embedding context to a *background*, a depthless plane. A recent commercial version is the high fashion frieze—again something that does not mimic nature—which splays pristinely costumed female figures flush against exotic slabs of nature where perhaps only goats and mendicants are actually to be found, nature here serving as a substitute for canvas.

(3) In portraiture, this transformation of contextual space into a point of focus and a flat background is matched by the transformation of microecological space. Self-commemoration by a kin group, team, school, or association packs familiars into compact rank-and-file clusters, graded for height; decorative kneeling and pyramiding can also be employed. This assures that a likeness of all the faces will show in the picture, along with at least an inferential view of the corresponding bodies, and all this as large as the camera can manage. In this bunching-up of models in order to take a picture, microecology and body contact are given a systematically different reading than obtains in any other frame, although the staging of choral singers comes close. Observe, I have been talking about real space between real people—models, not subjects. The current commercial version of group pictures presents an even more striking reconstitution of space, for it brings into jolly togetherness a deep-sea diver, a Chinese cook, a ballet dancer, a black nurse, a middle-age housewife, and a grey-haired banker, causing subjects whom all of social life conspires to keep separate to be arm in arm, nullifying the basic metaphor indexing social distance through interpersonal physical space. But, of course, there is a profound difference between commemoratives and commercials. Teammates who entwine themselves for a portrait produce a picture of themselves displaying this territorial promiscuity; professional models who similarly pose themselves do not produce a picture of themselves but of subjects chosen by advertiser, and it is the intermingling of subjects in the pictured space, not models in the studio's, that is striking. After all, professional models, like professional actors, have given up almost all natural claims and can be caused to appear in almost any guise and almost any posture.

(4) An individual who serves as a model for a personal portrait—or does anything else—is someone with a unique biographical individuality, allowing for a matching between

---

[18] In recent years stylish portrait photographers have broken with the traditional format. Instead of inducing frozen facial dignity in a model, they track down expressions of warmth, charm, liveliness, and so forth, producing a sense that the individual has been unself-consciously caught in action. To obtain these expressions, a considerable warm-up period may be employed and a second camera, so that the model will not quite know when and from what precise angle his image will be taken. In this way, every customer can be transformed into a fitting object for sympathetic, candid photography and high symbolism, becoming someone who expresses his character, as well as his status, allowing photographers to make a statement every time their camera speaks. It is through such practices that those who make a living reproducing appearances of life can continue further to stamp the real thing out.

[19] See, for example, Rubens' *Hélène Fourment in a Fur Coat*, and the discussion in Berger (1975:60-61). I might add that a whole art has developed in radio and TV to induce performers to project their talk as if to actual audiences located at some prescribed distance, and as if part of a current interaction. On the contingencies of training political candidates in these techniques, see Carey (1976).

subject and personal identity of the model, providing only that the model is known personally, or at least known *of,* by the viewer. (Thus the photographic game of identifying baby pictures or high school photos or of matching early pictures of celebrities against their current image.) For viewers of a portrait, this matching possibility is crucial; ritual use cannot be made of pictures of just anyone, only pictures of the famed or of those within one's own circle. In the case of commercial pictures, this linkage is unnecessary—except in regard to celebrity or "citizen" testimonials.

Observe that in photographic portraits, the model is frankly "posed." His having taken up a position before the camera simply in order to be photographed in no way detracts from the picture being thought an authentic, "real" one. Moreover, what is pictured is what is really going on, namely, portraiture, the giving of the model over to the process of being rendered. We would not say, then, that such a picture was "merely posed," as though to correct anyone's belief that it was something else. That the background may be a mere *picture* of scenery does not discredit the portrait either, for here there is no pretense that anything but a prop is involved.

One is reminded here of the frame complexity of apparently naive photographs and the diverse realms of being we seem able to easily amalgamate. For example, a photograph may involve not only a model who is a *real* person and a backdrop which is a *painting* of trees, but also a framed photograph or oil portrait, real in its own sense, used as a scenic resource, introducing still another plane of events. Indeed, at the turn of the century mortuary pictures were to be found in which a framed photographic portrait of the deceased was set amidst wreaths and real flowers, all placed in front of a cloudy canvas sky and photographed. (Incidentally, what resulted was a *photograph* of a photograph, something that is frame-distinct from a print off the same negative, the rephotograph of a photograph, and, of course, a letterpress reproduction of a photograph.) In all of these ways photographic portraiture has from the beginning involved embeddings of material from one frame into materials in another,[20] a practice, incidentally, long employed in painting.

A "real" photographic portrait may be one that strikes the viewer as bad in various ways: it may be unflattering or fail to capture the personality the model is "known" to have or be badly composed, lighted, printed, and so forth. But these deficiencies do not reflect on the genuineness or authenticity of the portrait. A question of fabrication and keying, a question of reality, would enter when we discovered that the portrait was "really" of someone else, merely someone who looked like the model we thought was involved or that the picture contained the mere posing of a posing, as when a commercial advertisement presents some-

thing meant to be seen as though a private photographic portrait when in fact a professional model did the work, posing in a way he would not were he posing for a photograph of himself for his own private use. To which must be added the fact that almost from the beginning of private personal photographic portraiture, models guyed the process, taking an avowedly "funny" picture, for example, one which extended the represented scenery into everything but a hole for the model's real head to be popped through, or one in which the model assumed a purposely comic pose. Commercial pictures then added a lamination, presenting pictures of professional models posed as private persons guying a portrait pose. I might add that when a genuine private photographic portrait is borrowed by a student, transformed into a slide, and presented to an audience as an instance of photographic portraiture, then one might have to say that although a real portrait is being used, it is not being used in the way intended, and no ritual attaches to its perception. Form remains; function changes.

Finally, look again at the notion of "posing." A commercial model staging an ad in which he is to appear as a doctor is "posing," an activity clearly different from "imposturing" as a doctor (as when someone attempts to practice medicine without training or a license), and akin to "acting" a medical role in a movie. But even more clearly, someone "posing" for his portrait is not doing so in the commercial model's sense. For, as suggested, in private portraits there is ordinarily no effort to use scenic cues to provide the viewer of the picture with an understanding that a make-believe world is pictured whose subjects have a social and personal identity little matching that of the models. Commercial posing avowedly transforms a model into almost anyone the advertiser wants to construct an imaginary scene around; private portraiture transforms a model into a decorative representation of himself, the two "ofs" of photography here nicely blended. Observe that the question of primping or posturing for the camera is not here at issue. Private portraiture, public portraiture for purposes of publicity, caught news shots of national leaders, and even art photography of "interesting looking" faces, all reflect the fundamental fact that their models are not presenting themselves in a personal or social identity not their "own"; that is what underlies our commonsense designation of these pictures as "actually of" their subjects. All are to be contrasted to commercial make-believe, whether fanciful or fully realistic, for whether a model poses as a doctor or Napoleon or the devil does not signify here; in all cases subject and model would not be the same, leading us to say that we do not have an *actual* picture *of* a doctor, Napoleon, or the devil. (Which is not to say that a model who poses as a doctor will not provide us with an actual *photograph*, nor an *actual* photograph *of* an adult, a male, a white person, a good-looker, a professional model, and so forth. Nor to deny that an actual photograph of a doctor is a possibility, whereas an actual photograph of Napoleon or the devil is not, although an actual photograph of an actual portrait of Napoleon is, whereas of the devil, not.)

VI It is apparent that the standards we bring to judging pictured scenes are not quite those we bring to judging picture portraits: of the first, is it doctored or

---

[20] Examples may be found in Lesy (1973). Postcards early in this century also employed embeddings, the beautiful beloved of the lonely lover appearing in a balloon above his head, ofttimes competing for free space with her photograph or portrait, this being a third realm employed, I suppose, in case the point was missed. Note, the equivalent of a thought balloon's access to the heated brain of a figure was a privilege of novelists before the camera was invented.

contrived, and in either case, covertly or overtly; of the second, is it "touched up," faithful, flattering, and the like. (Ordinary concerns usually neglect the possibility that what might seem to be a private portrait might really be the fabrication or keying of one, this neglect due, perhaps, to the fact that a portrait is already a keying, already a ritualization of the human form, already a departure from the simple rendering of an aspect of the world the way it is for us.) In any case, the question can be raised as to how, apart from portraiture, photographs can feature subjects in a way that is systematically different from the way their models might deploy themselves when not before a camera. Here, then, is a concern that does not bear on issues associated with the physiology and psychology of perception. In brief, what are the systematic differences between scenes openly contrived for picturing and live scenes whose participants are unconcerned about being photographed; or, put the other way, what are the systematic differences between pictures of openly contrived scenes and pictures of uncontrived ones?

(1) Perhaps the most obvious departure from reality that photography provides is commercial syncretism. The capacity to put together a realistic looking scene to photograph is not far away from the capacity to put together a scene whose individual elements are imaginable as real but whose combination of elements the world itself could not produce or allow. Thus fantastical pictures in which a subject speaks to us from within a block of ice or while soaring through the air, or mingles socially with figures from myth or with notables long since dead but now returned in their prime, or seriously displays ineptness, braggadocio, fearfulness, and hauteur we would only expect to find in conscious buffoonery, or is subjected to our reading his thoughts in a balloon that the other figures in the picture can't see. A more subtle complexity is found in those ads which intendedly satirize other ads, thus elevating the make-believe world portrayed in one picture into real materials to copy in the make-believe world of another, providing thus a keying of a keying.

(2) Consider now involvement structure. A feature of social situations is that participants are obliged to sustain appearances of spontaneous involvement in appropriate matters at hand. Evidence of an individual's involvement will come from the direction and mobility of his gaze, as well as the alignment of his eyes, head, and trunk, these ordinarily oriented in the same direction. Now it seems that of all obligatory appearances, that of correct involvement is the hardest to simulate, and this as if by design. Any attempt to produce an appropriate show of involvement in something tends to produce instead an appearance of involvement in the task of affecting such involvement.[21] Although most individuals acquire the capacity to convincingly contrive a show of interest in what another is saying or doing, ability falters when they are required to simulate "natural" involvement within more complex social arrangements, as when listening to talk that the talker is himself simulating, or expressing to one participant a shared reaction regarding another, or maintaining one conversation in very close proximity to another. At such moments the individual is

likely to induce a sense of uneasiness in viewers, due to the perceived overfixedness of his gaze and his failure to align trunk, head, and eyes in the manner we have come to expect. Perhaps the most obtrusive example is to be seen when an individual glances at a camera or persons monitoring him but tries to prevent his trunk and his head from following his eyes. May I add that our capacity to discern microscopic discrepancies in anticipated alignments of eyes, head, and trunk is simply enormous.

(3) Another sort of photographic departure from reality can be seen by contrasting portraits and scenes. It is clear that although an image of a person or even of a group of persons (if in staggered array) can be rather fully caught from the front by the camera's straight-on eye, the activity in natural social situations can rarely be well pictured from such an angle. Best vantage point must be chosen afresh for each configuration, and this can involve a positioning of the camera that an eye and its person could hardly manage in natural social life. More important, activity may have to be broken up and spread open, for a camera cannot peer inside the inward-facing encirclements often found. (After all, portrait posing is not a posture dictated by what can go on in social situations; it is through and through an answer to the special needs of the camera and to the character of portraiture.) And such a spread-out array can be staged to incorporate devices for directing the attention of the viewer to a central person, which devices do not otherwise appear in nature. Thus in political publicity shots, one practice is to have the leader's advisors and children turn their faces from the camera and self-effacingly look at the main figure, deictically pointing with their faces and sometimes their hands in the direction that attention is to follow, even while the central person waves directly to the camera and the crowd. All of this is found only where there is a front-on audience or a camera, and is radically different from the inward turning exhibited in ordinary face-to-face interaction.[22]

There are other instructive differences between portraits and pictured scenes. In both cases, the persons who model for the pictures have unique biographical (personal) identities. As suggested, for the owner of a photographic portrait, the possibility of making this identification is central to the ritual function the portrait will have. But not so in the case of commercial pictures, except perhaps when the picture features a personal testimonial.[23] Presumably

---

[21]See Goffman, "Alienation from Interaction" (1967:113-136).

---

[22]Other unnatural devices for exhibiting dominance are available to photographers. For example, a cliche of advertisements is to picture one individual who is in the close company of another looking at that other adoringly and self-effacingly, as if the other's use of the advertised product had rendered him worthy of such attention. Although openly loving looks at close quarters are sometimes addressed to the very young as part of their easy transformation into nonpersons, these expressions between adults are not common, being incompatible with other interaction obligations of the adorer to the adored.

[23]Portraits taken of anonymous models by renowned photographers can become prized by the collectors, and in this sense have ritual value, but here because the picture provides a contact with the taker, not the taken. There are, of course, various efforts to constitute photographs into objects of scarcity—into relics—and thereby into items of monetary value. Prints from the original negative are apparently distinguishable from re-photographs of the text. The skill involved in developing and enlarging can itself be claimed as identifiable and therefore a means of distinguishing products. Etc. (For all of which, and for much other help, I am grateful to Lee Ann Draud.)

what the advertisement is concerned to depict is not particular individuals already known, but rather activity which would be recognizable were we to see it performed in real life by persons not known to us personally. (Which is not to say that the subjects may not be depicted in a manner to imply that they would naturally know each other very well.) In effect, pictured scenes show examples of categories of persons, not particular persons. Now observe that although in real life we obtain lots of views of persons whom we can merely place in social categories, unless we also know them personally or have good business reasons to be dealing with them, we are not in a position to witness what we witness about them in commercial scenes. Indeed, there are many pictured scenes, such as that of husband and wife in their bedroom, that no business or acquaintanceship could warrant our seeing. Only a peeping tom of unprecedented capabilities could manage the view. Like readers of what a novelist supplies of his characters, the viewer becomes god-like, unconstrained by any need of legitimate social grounds for being privy to what is depicted in the scene.[24] In short, the possibility of arranging a scene from the visual pinpoint of view of a single camera's eye—into which angle and distance of vision vast hordes of viewers can be thrust—is a social license as well as an optical one.

(4) A feature of the photographic frame is the possibility of eschewing the depiction of ordinary life for high symbolism. Thus, an image of part of a model's body can be made to fill the whole picture, articulated to be read as a deep comment on the entire human condition, not merely an example drawn from it, and providing us with a picture whose subject is not a person but a small part of the anatomy, such as a fingertip. A lesser version of this expressionism must be considered, being more common and probably more significant.

In real situations, we externalize our circumstances and intent, in effect facilitating the adaptation of others in our surround to us. But in a manner of speaking, this display tends to occur as part of a stream of acts in the same order of being, some of which acts have just occurred and others of which are likely to start occurring. In private and publicity portraiture, individuals can be given a quite different relation to what they display. Two boxers taking weighing-in publicity shots will assume a fighting pose, choreographing an illustration of the actions they will engage in. But these actions are "mere" representations, totally cut off from any actual sequence in which the orginals might occur. And indeed, little competence in fistic arts is required to evince the pose. What we obtain are photographic recordings of emblems, not actions. Similarly, when a renowned scientist graciously submits to a magazine interview (in the interests of disseminating knowledge), he is likely to be posed fingering his equipment as though a slice of his occupational life had been caught: he is shown peering into a microscope, writing a formula on the board, holding a test tube up to the

light, or arranging a fossil. Thereby he crudely mimes a posture plucked from his own role, momentarily transforming the living tools of his trade into dramaturgic equipment and himself into a pantomimist of fixed expressions. And what we see is not a photographic record of an actual scene from the scientist's life, as would be available were a secret camera trained on his laboratory, nor a clever contrivance of such a photographic record (this presented either as a real one or as an admitted simulation), but something that is *only* to be found as a posing for a picture, having been staged in response to a conception of what would make a colorful, telling photograph, and, behind this, a conception of what constitutes the appropriate convention for "representing" the particular calling.[25] Obviously in all these cases what one has is not intention display in the ethological sense, since emblems of the model's calling do not tell us what is to happen (or what is threatened or promised), but rather the sort of activity the model chooses to be identified with, this activity being symbolized, as it were, by a quotation of one of its dramatically telling phases.[26] What in fact probably has happened is that the staff photographer has okayed the pose, and what probably will happen is that the scientist will soon exchange pleasantries with his departing guests—these events belonging to an order of activity radically different from the one intendedly portrayed in the picture.

VII It is plain, then, that except in the case of caught scenes, the arrangements of models and scenic resources that the camera photographs will differ systematically from the way the unposing world is. Now one should consider the contrary issue: the carryover of the way the world is to any photograph. For the transformational code for representing reality in pictures—the photographic frame—would hardly be a code were not some sort of relationship systematically preserved between what is transformed and the transformation. But in the question of carryover, some preliminary discussion is required.

Photographs (like pencil sketches) can be used to *illustrate*

---

[24] Cartoon strips provide other transformations of the everyday. For example, the protagonists can be at a distance or even hidden yet their words can be ballooned into the foreground, in effect allowing the viewer to bug distal voices. Here, and in regard to other aspects of the transformation rules of the cartoon frame, see Fresnault-Deruelle (1975a, 1975b, 1976).

[25] For this latter point, and for other suggestions incorporated without further acknowledgment, I am very grateful to John Carey.

[26] Scientists are here used as an example because one might think they would balk at such nonsense. Examples are even easier to find among business leaders who appear in news magazines and annual company reports busy with an executive-like action whose posing could only have taken them away from such duties. In truth it seems that nigh everyone can be persuaded by publicists to appear to the public at large in a mock-up of themselves and their occupations, an amateur theatrics to which politicians are also willing to subject their greetings, farewells, commiserations, and other intimacy rituals. Nor is this readiness to reframe one's own doings so that the public will get a synoptic view of one's role a particularly contemporary phenomenon. Bourgeois society has never wanted for persons ready to see the need for a permanent display of themselves in somber portrait oils, clutching a book, a ledger, a riding crop, or a rose, framing themselves thus in some sort of mystical relation to the equipment of their vocation, a touching encouragement to the worship that others might be willing to offer to exemplifications of what is best in humanity. Perhaps one should see the readiness for this sort of personal publicity as entirely natural to the self, and a modest life a perversion forced upon the masses for want of anything like an adequate supply of board rooms and marble fireplaces.

behavioral practices and arrangements, typically by virtue of models having been posed accordingly. The kind of practices photographs can best illustrate are those that are firmly codified as to form and can be represented from beginning to end, *in toto*, within the visual field that can be nicely encompassed by short-range camera focus.[27] Of course, one is likely to be interested in photographable behavioral practices because they are routinely associated with particular social meanings, and it is admittedly the sign vehicle, not the signification, that is precisely illustratable.

As I use the term "illustration," no implication is intended about existence; an illustrated practice may have occurred, but illustration itself does not attest to such occurrence, belonging to subjects, not models. It is, then, perfectly reasonable to expect that illustrations may be found across several modes of representation, some clearly involving make-believe. For example, the "arm-lock," the standard adult cross-sex tie-sign in our society, can be illustrated by means of what can be found in comics, cartoons, realistic ads, news shots of celebrities who are "on," two actors taking the part of a couple on the theatrical stage, caught pictures from ordinary life scenes, and, of course, live scenes. More to the point, across these quite different realms of being, no systematic relevant difference seems detectable in the armlocks depicted; the form of this display can be, and very often is, perfectly represented *in toto* in any of these frames.

Photographs can also be used to provide documentation or an *instance-record* of the sort of behavioral practice which can be illustrated pictorially. An instance-record is evidence (which a mere illustration is not) that an instance of the practice *did* occur as pictured on the occasion of the picture taking. Call such a picture an *instantiation*. Note that a picture which records an instance of a practice, that is, instantiates it, is necessarily a good illustration of it, something that can't be said of many other kinds of records. And observe that pictures can be used not merely to provide instance-records of practices already known, but also to help us become aware of practices theretofore unidentified.

Now note that if one's interest is in the picturing of scenes as well as in the scenes that are pictured, then the difference between illustration and instantiation can become complicated. For any photograph which merely illustrates a behavioral practice must also provide not merely an instance-record of the illustrative practice, but an instance itself. And the same can be said when one passes beyond illustration itself to *symbolization*, namely, a referencing based on what may be a loose, uncodified connection between sign and meaning (or a fixed but thoroughly conventional one), and upon an evoked significance which may bear little relation to the facts. A creditably candid wedding picture of the groom placing a ring on the finger of the bride not only attests reliably to a wedding having taken place, but also supplies us with a special segment of the ceremony, one that has come to serve as a symbol of the whole, and behind this, as a symbol of the presumably loving relationship that was solemnized on the occasion. In fact,

however, the pictured event itself does not provide us with evidence of the sequence of specific ritual details out of which the wedding in question was formulated, or evidence of the quality of the relationship thereby ratified. What can be instantiated in completed form (and what is therefore most suitable to pictorial research) involves lesser matters, such as the asymmetry of the traditional ring ritual, the general styling of wedding rings, and the choice of fingers thought proper for the placement of this piece of ceremonial jewelry. On the other hand, an "expressive" picture does provide an actual instance of the use in pictures of stereotyped symbolizations of wider social events and relationships.

The differences among illustrations, instance records, and symbolizations as here defined, complicate the analysis of pictures. A further bedevilment is the "photographic fallacy," namely, the very general tendency to confuse realness with representativeness and ideographic with nomothetic validity. A caught photograph of persons in action can provide all the evidence that one needs that a particular event—such as a wedding—very likely did occur. But that sufficiency is for those interested in the particulars of the past, in a word, biography. If instead one is interested in social routines, in customary behavioral patterns, then a wedding picture must differently figure; it can provide an instance record of, say, placement pattern with respect to the ring, but very little evidence concerning the social characteristics of the populations across which the practice is found and the range of contexts in which it occurs among these people—in fact, little evidence that one is dealing with a pattern at all. Yet when one establishes that a picture of something really is of the subject it portrays, it is very hard to avoid thinking that one has established something beyond this, namely, something about the event's currency, typicality, commonness, distribution, and so forth. The paradox is that "small behaviors" are what can be very fully instantiated by a single photograph, but one such picture can only establish the feasibility of actual occurrence. (The picture of Lee Harvey Oswald being shot provides excellent evidence of how a revolver was held on one occasion and, more important, Jack Ruby's guilt in this connection; but the picture provides little evidence of how hand guns are generally held for close range firing.) To which one must add that very often the sort of event whose *mere* occurrence—not *typicality* of occurrence—is of biographical or historic interest is one that cannot be photographed in the round throughout its course, but only in cross-section, as it were, this moment often providing very inadequate evidence of the occurrence and character of the event as a whole.

VIII Turn now to the question of carryover. Whether a pictured scene is caught, faked, or, in varying degrees realistically mocked-up, the model will bring elements of himself to it, affording to the viewers something of what he affords the eyes of actual participants in his real scenes. Just as a stage actor (but not an opera singer) can hardly perform a part in a language other than one in which he has a real competence, so models, professional or amateur, cannot transform themselves completely for a photographic appearance, at least if they are not to be encumbered with a

---

[27] For example, tongue showing: Smith, Chase, and Lieblich (1974).

massive disguise. In theory at least, personal identity will be recoverable, ofttimes also the unique setting in which the photograph occurred (if not by us, then by modeling agencies, the police, kinsmen of the models, or whoever). However, if our interests are not ritualistic, as when we cherish a picture of Aunt Mabel because she herself can be identified in it, or legalistic, as when we establish that the person a certificate authorizes is the person who is presenting the authorization, or playful, as when we match early portraits against later ones, but rather academic, namely, to inquire into the way the world is, then identifiability as such ceases to be central.

Other matters will be more important. We are all in our society trained to employ a somewhat common idiom of posture, position, and glances, wordlessly choreographing ourselves relative to others in social situations with the effect that interpretability of scenes is possible. Some of this idiom we automatically continue to employ in composing and posing for scenes that are to be photographed—jumbled up, of course, with crude patches of gross symbolization for the camera.

But that is only the beginning, for however posed and "artificial" a picture is, it is likely to contain elements that record instances of real things. The scene pictured on the backdrop of a photographic portrait might be a painted fantasy, but the chair the subject sits on is real enough and speaks to a real genre of chairs, not pictures. (Students question the sense in which a chair can be said to be real, but *that* sort of doubt is not here at issue, for however that question is answered, the fact still remains that a picture of a chair is a radically different thing from a chair itself.) The clothes worn on the occasion are often Sunday best, sometimes causing the wearer to feel "unnatural," but, of course, in all likelihood there will be real ceremonial occasions when the same garb will have been worn, the limiting case here being the wedding gown, since it may be worn and pictured on the same and (often) only occasion. The way a female model for a seated private portrait manages her legs can be a very studied effect helped along sometimes by the photographer, but what the two here strive for in this apparently artificial way can be exactly what she strives for when seated at a party facing viewers from the front; what one is learning about, then, is how she might choreograph herself for front views in general, not for camera views in particular. The same can be said for the Western male practice of covering the crotch when in a sitting position. The fact that male subjects from non-Western cultures tend not to exhibit this protectiveness in portraits is not a specific difference between their pictures and ours, merely an incidental one, being specific to the more general issue of behavior when exposed to direct view, and pertains to models, not merely subjects. When a movie starlet couple at a nightclub back bench suddenly adjust their faces into the stylized teeth grimace found mainly in photographs, doing this because a cameraman has come into sight, the free distance between their rumps can still reflect spacing practices in uncontrived scenes, not merely contrived ones—although admittedly in photographs indexed distances and especially depths are hard to measure. And by examining the spacing and body orientation of the two in regard to other subjects in the picture, we come to take it for granted,

probably quite correctly, that the two constitute a "with," drawing here on precisely the same cues we would automatically employ when functioning as actual participants of live scenes.

IX Given that pictures may be organized as portraits or as scenes (and if the latter, caught, faked, or realistic to a degree), and given the distinction between illustration and instantiation, and the contrast of both of these to evocative symbolizations providing at best a purely conventional relation between vehicle and sign, and given further that one can be concerned about the nature of pictures as well as the nature of the world, it is possible to begin to see how heterogeneous a photograph may be as an object of academic interest.

One finds in pictures not only rules of scene production that are exclusive to pictures, but also photographic conventions peculiar to particular subject matters. For example, portrait photographers routinely touch up negatives or prints to improve the complexion of the subjects appearing in them, creating a people that has smoother skin than that found among mortals. In ads brunette women tend to be styled somewhat differently from blond women; this presumably a characteristic of pictures, not life.[28]

The settings in which members of a family snap one another are not fabricated for the purpose, are not merely props, but, as with the real settings used in home movies,[29] are hardly a haphazard selection from all the ones the family employs, and can only have the effect of producing a false general impression of its habitat. The expensive backdrops found in most commercial scenes *can* be found in the real world but only in very narrow circles. (Once rented or donated as background for a film or an advertisement, these environments can become merely another element of the world to which the viewer has pictorial access; they can become unrealistically familiar.) The females depicted in commercially posed scenes have straighter teeth and are slimmer, younger, taller, blonder, and "better" looking than those found in most real scenes, even most real scenes occurring in stylish settings, but certainly these figures are similar to the ones found in uncontrived, live scenes that occur in modeling agencies and other real places where mainly models foregather—which places, note, may not be luxuriously furnished. In contrast, the fact that women in American advertisements show no hair on their legs or under their arms can be taken to reflect directly the shaving

---

[28] Suggested in Millum (1975:142).

[29] See Chalfen (1975:96). Commercial movies can be shot in a studio containing hand-fashioned environments, or on an open studio lot, or in a geographical region that is similar in terrain to the real thing but closer to hand, or "on location" where the fictive events are purported to occur. But "real" in the last case must be used with care. Because mocked-up events are staged in these settings, often set in an epoch before or after the actual moviemaking, and because the ordinary traffic of people and events must be roped off during shooting, the realism provided by the setting can only serve to heighten the illusion, as when a con man manages to make use of a real banking office to hoodwink a mark. Reliance on such backdrops to establish life-likeness gives them a significance different from what they would ordinarily have, transforming them—as far as function is concerned—into quotations or symbols of themselves.

practice prevalent among women throughout America. (But the hairless legs and armpits displayed in French advertisements *cannot* similarly be taken as evidence of appearances beyond the camera, for in France, American depilatory practices so far have mostly influenced the commercially pictured world.) Finally, the general difference in hair styling, facial decoration, and clothing pattern that distinguishes male subjects from female subjects in American advertisements is by and large true of how males in all Westernized countries are distinguished from females both in posings for advertisements and in uncontrived scenes. To which must be added that what is common to commercial scenes and rare in life may yet be commonly part of the ideals and fantasies of many actual people.

In sum, between commercially posed scenes and live ones there is every kind of carryover and almost every kind of discrepancy. Nor are matters in any way fixed. As soon as a formulaic feature of commercially choreographed scenes is uncovered and publicized, advertisers are in a position to self-consciously initiate a sharply contrary policy or to present guyed versions of the old. Withal, the art of analysis is to begin with a batch of pictures and end up with suggestions of unanticipated features of uncontrived scenes, or with representations of themes that are hard to write about but easy to picture, or with illustrations of novel differences between pictures and life. And throughout, I believe, the issue of exploration should be kept separate temporally from the issue of proof. Arrangements which hold for many live scenes (or many pictured ones) lie ready to be uncovered in one example, but not direct evidence concerning their actual distribution.

X   Finally, another look at the notion of a "scene," along with a review of the concept of commercial realism.

Consider first the organizational constraints all scenes in advertisements might share and presuppose, and the liberties that can (but aren't necessarily) taken in their assembly; in short, consider the realm of being of which the drama in every individual ad is but an instance.

It is easy to contrast what goes on in ads to what goes on in the real world and conclude—as commentators are wont—that advertisements present a dolled-up, affluent version of reality, but this does not tell us about the structure of advertising's world, that is, the way in which it is put together. So, too, it is easy to see commercial realism as constituting but another make-believe realm (along with the theater, cartoons, the novel, etc.) and to contrast all these merely fictive domains with reality; but however instructive, this comparison, I think, misses the point. For although such a contrast ought to be made, there is another that should precede it. To explicate commercial realism one must start with the notion of "scene," *whether live or fictive*, and only after scenes have been contrasted to other ways of organizing understanding should, I think, one go on to contrast the commercially depicted variety in pictures to live, uncontrived ones.

The term "scene" is itself not a particularly happy one. An actual view, or a picture of a view, of something that is relatively unchanging—like a forest or a skyline—is called a scene, as is any background or backdrop, however bustling,

which a playwright or novelist might want to set as the general context of his action. A segment of an act in a stage play (something an act may have anywhere from one to ten of, each offering continuous action in one place) is also called a scene. A quarrel between related persons, conducted in a manner sensed to be open by onlookers to whom the disputants are less related, is also called a scene. And there is a current vernacular use, referring to something that an individual might make, dig, or dislike. The scenes this paper has been concerned with are of a different order.

In actual life as we wend our way through our day we pass into and out of immediate perception range of sequences of others; fleeting opportunity for viewing also occurs when they pass us. In metropolitan circumstances this means that we will be momentary onlookers of those whom we cannot identify biographically through name or appearance, that is, that we will catch glimpses of courses of action of strangers. Due to the warranted reputation of various behavioral settings and to the conventions of self-presentation, we will be able to infer something about the social identity (age, sex, race, class, etc.) of these strangers, their personal relationship to one another, their mood, and their current undertakings, these last, typically, only broadly categorized.

The totality of viewings of the courses of action of strangers which we obtain throughout our days constitutes our glimpsed world. This is not quite an impersonal world, especially for sophisticated viewers. But it is a truncated one, and one in which almost everything can be located in broad categories only. It is ordinarily bereft of details concerning the lives of those who are witnessed in passing and bereft of their longitudinal point of view regarding what they are seen as being and doing. (We strangers do not see John and Mary comparison shopping for a brooch to replace the one that was lost last week at Jean's party, nor do we detect that their apparent dallying is due to their having to kill some time before going on to catch the new Fellini. That is what they see. We see a young middle-class couple looking at things in a jewelry store.) Observe, then, that to glimpse a world is not somehow to happen upon an intimate revealing drama that was not meant for us. Nor is it to obtain a somehow marred, distorted, fragmentary view of the whole, something that can be caused to snap back into its proper shape by the addition of new information or the exercise of interpretive skill. It is not as though we were cryptographers having to start with a partially deciphered text, able to take comfort in the prospect of eventual success in unlocking what has all along been there. Or cardiologists interpreting the sounds of a stethoscope for the character of a patient's disease. To glimpse a world rather is to employ a set of categories more or less distinctive to glimpsing and often entirely adequate for the job they are designed to do. Nor are these categories rough and undeveloped; indeed, the persons glimpsed are likely to be quite aware of precisely how they can be read, and will have as part of their concern to conform to anticipated displayings of themselves and to use these behavioral rubrics as a cover behind which to pursue all manner of unpublishable projects. Yet no amount of supplementary information of the kind we are likely to obtain is likely to bring us to the private view that the objects of our attention will themselves have of their own undertakings. To be sure, our passing views as strangers and the sustained views of participants are not usually contradictory, and rough correspondences could be worked out, but inevitably our concerns and theirs will be considerably different, as to a degree will be the world their conventional public behavior generates for us and the world they are in while moving from point to point under these ensigns.

Now although there are real individuals whose glimpsed world is almost their only one, most of us live, and principally, in other worlds, ones having a longitudinal character, featuring extended courses of interlinked action and unique relationships to other people. Observe that a stage play or even a comic strip provides us with something quite beyond a glimpse of the lives (albeit fictional lives) of its characters; for we are given considerable personal information about the protagonists and can link together various glimpsings of them, in consequence of which we can enter into their courses of action in more detail and with much more temporal depth than is ordinarily possible in the case of our real passing views of the lives of strangers.

Commercial realism (along with certain cartoons and other drawings) provides, then, something of the same sort of realm as the one a stranger to everyone around him really lives in. The realm is full of meaningful viewings of others, but each view is truncated and abstract in the ways mentioned.

And now having noted the significant similarity between live scenes and the ones pictured in advertisements, one can go on to properly locate the consideration already given of differences. To repeat: glimpses of real life (like caught photographs of it) provide us with models who are portraying themselves, whereas commercial realism does not—cartoons and other drawings may not even employ models. Yet there are ways in which commercial realism provides us something that is fuller and richer than real glimpses. First, ads (along with cartoons and other one-shot drawings) are intentionally choreographed to be unambiguous about matters that uncontrived scenes might well be uninforming about to strangers. Second, scenes contrived for photographing (just as the ones drawn in comics) can be shot from any angle that the cameraman chooses, the subjects themselves splayed out to allow an unobstructed view; these are two liberties that a person viewing a live scene cannot take. Finally, short of engaging in voyeuristic activity, a real person is very considerably restricted as to the sorts of live scenes he will be allowed to glimpse from whatever angle, for his presence in a place always requires social warrant. In advertised worlds, however, we can look in on almost everything. Observe that these dramaturgic advantages of commercial realism over real life, other fictional realms have also, along with some advantages that commercial realism lacks.

A closing comment. The magical ability of the advertiser to use a few models and props to evoke a life-like scene of his own choosing is not primarily due to the art and technology of commercial photography; it is due primarily to those institutionalized arrangements in social life which allow strangers to glimpse the lives of persons they pass, and to the readiness of all of us to switch at any moment from dealing with the real world to participating in make-believe ones.

REFERENCES CITED

Barthes, Roland
  1972 Mythologies. Annette Lavers, trans. New York: Hill and Wang.
Berger, John
  1975 Ways of Seeing. London: Pelican.
Carey, John
  1976 A Micro-Frame Analysis of the On-Camera/On-Mike Paralinguistic Behavior of Three Presidential Candidates. Ph.D. dissertation, Annenberg School of Communications, University of Pennsylvania.
Chalfen, Richard
  1975 Cinéma Naiveté: A Study of Home Moviemaking as Visual Communication. Studies in the Anthropology of Visual Communication 2:87-103.
Fresnault-Deruelle, Pierre
  1975a La couleur et l'espace dans les comics. Documents de Travail #40, Series F. Centro Internazionale di Semiotica e di Linguistica, Università di Urbino d'Italia.
  1975b L'espace interpersonnel dans les comics. In Semiologié de la Représentation. André Helbo, ed. Pp. 129-150. Brussels: Editions Complexe.
  1976 Du linéaire au tabulaire. Communications 24:7-21.
Goffman, Erving
  1967 Interaction Ritual. New York: Anchor.
  1974 Frame Analysis. New York: Harper and Row.
Goodman, Nelson
  1968 Languages of Art. New York: Bobbs-Merrill.
Lesy, Michael
  1973 Wisconsin Death Trip. New York: Pantheon.
Livingston, Victor
  1976 Are the Nuns in This Ad What They Appear to Be? The Evening Bulletin (Philadelphia), March 11.
Millum, Trevor
  1975 Images of Women: Advertising in Women's Magazines. London: Chatto and Windus.
Smith, W. John, Julia Chase, and Anna Katz Lieblich
  1974 Tongue Showing: A Facial Display of Humans and Other Primate Species. Semiotica 11(3):201-246.
Van Dormael, Monique
  1974 The Photoroman Frame. Unpublished paper, University of Pennsylvania.

GENDER COMMERCIALS

I Reproduced in this chapter are some commercial still photographs—ads—featuring human subjects. In addition, some use is made of news shots of "actual" persons, that is, of models who are being pictured in their own capacity. My assumption is that anyone whose picture appears in media print has almost certainly cooperated in the process and therefore—like a professional model—has placed this appearance in the public domain, foregoing the protection from social analysis that persons, at least living ones, can strongly claim regarding pictures taken for home consumption.

The pictures reproduced were selected at will from newspapers and current popular magazines easy to hand—at least to my hand.[1] They were chosen to fit into sets, each set to allow the displaying, delineating, or mocking up of a discrete theme bearing on gender, especially female gender, and arranged with malice within each set to the same end. Each set of pictures is accompanied informally by some verbal text.

II Some comments first concerning how pictures can and can't be used in social analysis. My claim is that the themes that can be delineated through pictures have a very mixed ontological status and that any attempt to legislate as to the order of fact represented in these themes is likely to be optimistic.

(1) The student of commercial pictures can draw a random sample from a magazine's particular issue, or from a defined period of issue, or from a specified list of magazines, and disclaim characterizing other issues, periods, or magazines, even more so other sources of pictures, such as newsprint, postcards, and the like, not even to mention actual life itself. Specifiable representativeness, then, is a way that a collection of pictures could qualify[2]—and a way the pictures about to be analyzed do not. (Of course, findings based on a systematic sample very often get their weight from the fact that the reader can be trusted to generalize the findings beyond their stated universe, statistical warrant for which would require another study, which, if done, would induce a still broader overgeneralization, and so on, but that is another matter.) Observe that this sort of representativeness pertains to pictures as such and doesn't tell us what we very often want to know, namely, what aspects of

---

[1] And to that of a fellow student, Michi Ishida.

[2] For a recent example, see Robinson (1976).

real life pictures provide us a fair image of, and what social effect commercial picturing has upon the life that is purportedly pictured—a limitation also of the purposely selected pictures displayed here.

(2) Since there is little constraint on what I elect to identify as a theme (a "genderism"), or which pictures I bring together in order to display what is thus identified, or on the way I order the stills within a given series, it could be taken that anything could be depicted that I can manage to suggest through what appears to be common to a few pictures. Success here requires nothing more than a small amount of perversity and wit and a large batch of pictures to choose from. The larger the initial collection, the more surely the analyst can find confirming examples of what he thinks he has found in one picture or would in any case like to depict—a case of representativeness declining as the data base increases. So effective depiction of a theme cannot in itself prove anything about what is found in pictures or, of course, in the world. Indeed, something like the method I use is employed by artful compilers of photographic funny books, camera pranksters who match gesticulatory pictures of famous citizens against animals and plants apparently engaged in similarly characterizable postures, or who superimpose ballooned thoughts and statements, these formulated to define the situation as it never was in actual life, committing the protagonists to responses of a wildly scurrilous kind. So, too, the texts accompanying the pictures are cast in the style of generalization-by-pronouncement found in the writings of freelance body linguists, strayed ethologists, and lesser journalists.

(3) The particular matters I want to consider raise three distinct and general methodological questions that should not be confused: discovery, presentation, and proof. Only the first two will here be at issue, these two allowing me to exploit without a major research investment the very special advantages of working with photographs, which advantages are as follows:

(i) There is a class of behavioral practices—what might be called "small behaviors"—whose physical forms are fairly well codified even though the social implications or meaning of the acts may have vague elements, and which are realized in their entirety, from beginning to end, in a brief period of time and a small space. These behavioral events can be recorded and their image made retrievable by means of audio and video tapes and camera. (Tape and film, unlike a still, provide not only a recoverable image of an actual instance of the activity in question, but also an appreciable collection of these records. More important, audio and video recordings of very small behaviors facilitate micro-functional study, that is, an examination of the role of a bit of behavior in the stream which precedes, co-occurs, and follows.) The coincidence of a subject matter and a recording technology places the student in an entirely novel relation to his data, forming the practical basis for microanalysis. This special research situation should not be confused with the use of recording technology to document a news story, provide a feel for a community, limn in the contours of a relationship, depict the history of a nation, or any other matter whose meaning is not linked to a fixed physical form which can be realized in the round in a recordable space and time.

(ii) Pictures from any source are now cheap and easy to

reproduce in uniform slide form. A collection allows for easy arranging and rearranging, a search and mock-up, trial and error juggling, something between cryptography and doing jigsaw puzzles, a remarkable aid both to uncovering patterns and finding examples, whether mere illustrations or actual instance records.

(iii) The student can exploit the vast social competency of the eye and the impressive consensus sustained by viewers. Behavioral configurations which he has insufficient literary skill to summon up through words alone, he can yet unambiguously introduce into consideration. His verbal glosses can serve as a means to direct the eye to what is to be seen, instead of having to serve as a full rendition of what is at issue. The notion of a "merely subjective response" can then be academically upgraded; for clearly part of what one refrains from studying because the only approach is through verbal vagaries has a specific nature and is precisely perceived, the vagary being a characteristic of one's literary incapacity, not one's data.[3]

(iv) A set of pictorial examples (whether illustrations or instance records) of a common theme provides more than a device for making sure that the pattern in question will be clear to the viewer. Often one or two examples would suffice for that. Nor does the size of the set relate to the traditional sampling notion of showing how prevalent were cases of a particular kind in the sample and (by extension) in the sampled universe. Something else is involved. Different pictorial examples of a single theme bring different contextual backgrounds into the same array, highlighting untold disparities even while exhibiting the same design. It is the depth and breadth of these contextual differences which somehow provide a sense of structure, a sense of a single organization underlying mere surface differences, which sense is not generated simply by reference to the numerical size of the set relative to the size of the sample. Whereas in traditional methods the differences between items that are to be counted as instances of the same thing are an embarrassment, and are so in the degree of their difference, in pictorial pattern analysis the opposite is the case, the casting together of these apparent differences being what the analysis is all about. Indeed, something is to be learned even when an advertiser in effect performs analysis backwards, that is, starts with the same models and the same sales pitch and then searches out different possible scenes as vehicles for them and it—all this in the hope of building product interest through a mixture of repetition and novelty. For in purposely setting out to ring changes on a set theme, the advertiser must nonetheless satisfy scene-production requirements such as propriety, understandability, and so forth, thereby necessarily demonstrating that, and how, different ingredients can be choreographed to "express" the same theme. Here, certainly, it is entirely an artifact of how advertisements are assembled that a set of them will exhibit a common underlying pattern, and here the student is only uncovering what was purposely implanted to this end in the first place. But how the advertiser succeeds in finding different guises for his stereotypes still instructs in the matter of how the materials of real scenes can be selected and shaped to provide a desired reading.

(4) The pictures I have un-randomly collected of gender-relevant behavior can be used to jog one's consideration of three matters: the gender behavioral styles found in actual life, the ways in which advertisements might present a slanted view thereof, and the scene-production rules specific to the photographic frame. Although my primary interest is actual gender behavior, the pictures are accompanied by textual glosses that raise questions of any order that might be stimulated by the pictures. In any case, what will mostly be shown and discussed is advertisers' views of how women can be profitably pictured. My unsubstantiated generalizations have the slight saving grace that they mostly refer to the way gender is pictured, not the way it is actually performed.

(5) By and large, I did not look for pictures that exhibited what seemed to me to be common to the two sexes, whether just in pictures or in reality as well. Nor for pictures that dealt with sex differences which I assumed were widely and well-understood. The vast amount of what is—at least to me—unremarkable in advertisements is thus vastly underrepresented. (Something of the same bias actually informs every ethnography; it is differences from one's own world and unexpected similarities that get recorded.) *But given these limitations, once a genderism was identified as one worth mocking-up, almost all sex role exceptions and reversals I came across were selected.* It is to be added that although the advertising business is focused (in the U.S.A.) in New York, and although models and photographers are drawn from a very special population indeed, their product is treated as nothing-out-of-the-ordinary by viewers, something "only natural." In brief, although the pictures shown here cannot be taken as representative of gender behavior in real life or even representative of advertisements in general or particular publication sources in particular, one can probably make a significant negative statement about them, namely, that *as pictures* they are not perceived as peculiar and unnatural. Also, in the case of each still, by imagining the sexes switched and imagining the appearance of what results, one can jar oneself into awareness of stereotypes. By keeping this switching task in mind, the reader can generate his own glosses and obtain a cue to the possible merit of mine.

(6) A further caveat. Advertisements overwhelmingly and candidly present make-believe scenes, the subjects or figures depicted being quite different from the professional models who pose the action. Obviously, then, a statement about, say, how nurses are presented in ads is to be taken as a shorthand way of saying how models dressed like nurses and set in a mock-up of a medical scene are pictured. (A fee could persuade a real nurse to pose in an ad about nursing or

---

[3] The ear as well as the eye provides an impressive competency, and here phoneticians (and lately those interested in conversational analysis) have made an exemplary effort to formulate notation systems that can be printed on paper yet avoid the limitations of ordinary orthography, thus providing a bridge between sounds and publications. The problem is that although trained students can produce the same transcription of a given spate of sound, the formulation they produce will equally apply to expressions which they would hear as significantly different. Given a recording to listen to, a linguist's transcription can serve as a very adequate means of directing the ear's attention to a particular sound and with that the full competency of the ear can be academically exploited. But written transcriptions without recordings do not solve the problem. (Nor, I believe, does it help much to package a tape in the jacket of a book, along with encouragement of do-it-yourself analysis.) The printing of the analysis of videotape records presents still greater problems.

allow a "caught" photograph of her in action to be used, but ordinarily advertising agencies find that a real nurse in a real hospital unsatisfactorily typifies her kind.) I will on occasion employ this simplification, speaking of the subjects of a picture as though they were instantiations, namely, recorded images of the real thing. The complication is that posing for an ad almost invariably involves a carryover of sex, female models appearing as female figures, and male models as males. (So, too, there is a carryover of broad ranges of age-grade.) It follows that any discussion of the treatment of gender in ads happens to strike where a sense is to be found in which model and subject are one. In statements about sex-stereotyping, then, there is special warrant for falling back upon simplified reference. An advertiser's contrived scene featuring a "nurse" does not present us with a photographic record of a nurse, that is, an *actual* picture *of* a real nurse, but nonetheless presents us with one of a real woman, at least in the common sense meaning of "real."[4] After the studio session is over, the model does not go on being a "nurse," but she does continue to be a "woman."

(7) Finally, a word about the arrangement of pictures in each series and other details. In general, subject matter proceeds from children to adults and from actual pictures to overtly contrived commercial ones. (An implication is thus implanted that ritualized behavioral practices found in a variety of contexts in real life come to be employed in a "hyper-ritualized" form in ads featuring women.) Depictions disconfirming the arrangements argued here, i.e., depictions of sex role reversals, are placed at the very ends of the series to which they belong and are marked off with a special border. It should also be noted that throughout females in a "feminine" stance will be seen to take up this position relative to another *woman*, not merely relative to a man, strongly suggesting that gender stereotypes—at least photographic ones—involve a two-slot format, the important issue being to fill the slots with role differentiated subjects, not necessarily with subjects of opposing sexual identity.

The pictures themselves have all been reproduced in black and white for reasons of cost. Although it would have been somewhat more accurate to reproduce the color ones in color, I feel that not much has been lost. Each picture has been numbered, and the numbers correspond to those appearing before the relevant verbal text; the text itself immediately precedes the series of illustrations to which it refers. Pictures as well as text have been footnoted, and pictures as well as text appear in footnotes. The photographs have been arranged to be "read" from top to bottom, column to column, across the page.

III Having considered reasons why my selection of commercial pictures need not be taken seriously, I want to consider some reasons why they should.

The task of the advertiser is to favorably dispose viewers to his product, his means, by and large, to show a sparkling version of that product in the context of glamorous events.

The implication is that if you buy the one, you are on the way to realizing the other—and you should want to. Interestingly, a classy young lady is likely to be in the picture adding her approval of the product and herself to its ambience, whether the product be floor mops, insecticides, orthopedic chairs, roofing materials, credit cards, vacuum pumps, or Lear jets. But all of this is only advertising and has little to do with actual life. So goes the critical view of these exploitive arts. Which view is itself naive, failing to appreciate what actual life has to do with.

Whatever point a print advertiser wants to make about his product, he must suffer the constraints of his medium in making it. He must present something that will be meaningful, easily so, yet all he has space to work with will be type and one or two still photographs, typically containing protagonists whose words (if any seem to be spoken) are unavailable. And although textual material outside of the picture brackets will provide a reading of "what is happening," this is commonly a somewhat duplicated version; the picture itself is designed to tell its little story without much textual assistance.

How can stills present the world when in the world persons are engaged in courses of action, in doings through time (not frozen posturings), where sound is almost as important as sight, and smell and touch figure as well? Moreover, in the world, we can know the individuals before us personally, something unlikely of pictures used in advertising.

Some of the solutions to this problem are obvious. A scene can be simulated in which figures are captured in those acts which stereotypically epitomize the sequence from which they are taken—presumably because these acts are identified as happening only in the course of, and momentarily during, an extended action. Thus viewers are led to read backward and forward in sequence time from the moment of vision.[5] Another solution is to draw on scenes that are themselves silent and static in real life: sleeping, pensive poses, window shopping, and, importantly, the off-angle fixed looks through which we are taken to convey our overall alignment to what another person—one not looking at us directly—is saying or doing. Another solution is to position the characters in the picture microecologically so that their placement relative to one another will provide an index of mapping of their presumed *social* position relative to one another. And, of course, there is the use of scenes and characters which have come to be stereotypically identified with a particular kind of activity by the widest range of viewers, thus ensuring instantaneous recognizability. Incidentally, advertisers overwhelmingly select positive, approved typifications (perhaps so their product will be associated with a good world as opposed to being dissociated from a bad one), so that what we see are idealized characters using ideal facilities to realize ideal ends—while, of course, microecologically arranged to index ideal relationships. Finally, advertisers can use celebrities as models, for although these personages are not known personally they are known about.

---

[4] Qualifications regarding the phrase "real woman" are presented in Goffman (1974:284-285).

[5] A point suggested to me some years ago by David Sudnow (see Sudnow 1972).

Interestingly, it is not merely commercial advertisers who have recourse to these pictorial methods. Governments and nonprofit organizations employ the same devices in order to convey a message through pages, posters, and billboards; so do radical groups and so do private persons with photography as a hobby or a calling. (It is rather wrong, alas, to say that only advertisers advertise. Indeed, even those concerned to oppose commercial versions of the world must pictorialize their arguments through images which are selected according to much the same principles as those employed by the enemy.)

I want to argue now that the job the advertiser has of dramatizing the value of his product is not unlike the job a society has of infusing its social situations with ceremonial and with ritual signs facilitating the orientation of participants to one another. Both must use the limited "visual" resources available in social situations to tell a story; both must transform otherwise opaque goings-on into easily readable form. And both rely on the same basic devices: intention displays, microecological mapping of social structure, approved typifications, and the gestural externalization of what can be taken to be inner response. (Thus, just as a Coca-Cola ad might feature a well-dressed, happy looking family at a posh beach resort, so a real family of modest means and plain dress might step up their level of spending during ten days of summer vacation, indeed, confirming that a self-realizing display is involved by making sure to photograph themselves onstage as a well-dressed family at a posh summer resort.) This is not to deny, of course, that the displays presented in stills are not a special selection from displays in general. Advertisers, by and large, must limit themselves to soundless, scentless appearances and one-shot moments of time, whereas actual ritual need not be restricted in these particular ways.

Which raises the issue of "social situations," defining these as arrangements in which persons are physically present to one another. Stills may, and often do, contain a solitary figure, ostensibly not in a social situation at all. But if the scene is to be read by the viewer, then the subject must give appearances and engage in doings that are informative, and these informings are just what we employ in actual social situations in order to establish our own stories and learn about the stories established by others. Solitary or not, figures in stills implicitly address themselves to us, the viewers, locating us close at hand through our being allowed to see what we can see of them, thus generating a social situation in effect. And indeed, the photographer often clinches matters by requiring solitary subjects to simulate a gestural response to a phantom hovering near the camera, a forcible reminder of the place we the viewers are supposed to inhabit. Observe, the solitary subject not only "externalizes" information that will give us an understanding of what it is that can be taken to be going on, but also quite systematically fails to exhibit taboo and unflattering self-involving behavior, even though these are just the sort of acts that are likely to occur when the actor is assured he is alone. (So perhaps a byproduct of commercial realism will be the reinforcement of censored versions of solitary conduct.)

When one looks, then, at the presentation of gender in advertisements, attention should be directed not merely to uncovering advertisers' stereotypes concerning the differences between the sexes—significant as these stereotypes might be. Nor only examine these stereotypes for what they might tell us about the gender patterns prevalent in our society at large. Rather one should, at least in part, attend to how those who compose (and pose for) pictures can choreograph the materials available in social situations in order to achieve their end, namely, the presentation of a scene that is meaningful, whose meaning can be read at a flash. For behind these artful efforts one may be able to discern how mutually present bodies, along with nonhuman materials, can be shaped into expression. And in seeing what picture-makers can make of situational materials, one can begin to see what we ourselves might be engaging in doing. Behind infinitely varied scenic configurations, one might be able to discern a single ritual idiom; behind a multitude of surface differences, a small number of structural forms.

Let me admit that these arguments about the relation of ritual to commercial pictures might seem to be a way of making the best of a bad thing, namely, using easily available ads to talk about actual gender behavior. But I am not interested here in behavior in general, only in the displays that individuals manage to inject into social situations, and surely this is part of what advertisers try to inject into the scenes they compose around the product and then photograph. Commercial pictures are in the main entirely posed, "mere pictures," at best "realistic." But, of course, the reality they presumably reflect distortedly is itself, in important ways, artificial. For the actuality here at issue is how social situations are employed as the scenic resource for constructing visually accessible, instantaneous portraits of our claimed human nature. Posed pictures can therefore turn out to be more substantial than one might have thought, being for students of a community's ritual idiom something like what a written text is for students of its spoken language.

Relative Size

1–4   One way in which social weight—power, authority, rank, office, renown—is echoed expressively in social situations is through relative size, especially height. This congruence is somewhat facilitated among males through occupational selection favoring size—a form of circularity, since selection often occurs in social situations where size can be an influence. In the case of interaction between parents and their young children, biology itself assures that social weight will be indexed by the physical kind.

In social interaction between the sexes, biological dimorphism underlies the probability that the male's usual superiority of status over the female will be expressible in his greater girth and height. Selective mating then enters to ensure that very nearly every couple will exhibit a height difference in the expected direction, transforming what would otherwise be a statistical tendency into a near certitude. Even in the case of mere clusters of persons maintaining talk, various forms of occupational, associational, and situational selection markedly increase the biologically grounded possibility that every male participant will be bigger than every female participant.

Now it seems that what biology and social selection facilitate, picture posing rigorously completes:

Indeed, so thoroughly is it assumed that differences in size will correlate with differences in social weight that relative size can be routinely used as a means of ensuring that the picture's story will be understandable at a glance:

2

He said:
I found the little black and white TV set in my bathroom, but can't find my big color set.

We said:
It's in that big armoire in your bedroom, sir. Along with a fold-out writing desk.

He said:
That big chest? Very clever.

We said:
Thank you sir. We thought you'd rather not have that big TV eye staring at you all the time.

3

5–7   And here exceptions seem to prove the rule. For on the very few occasions when women are pictured taller than men, the men seem almost always to be not only subordinated in social class status, but also thoroughly costumed as craft-bound servitors who—it might appear—can be safely treated totally in the circumscribed terms of their modest trade:

5

The "typical" American driver:

6

The most irresistible Valentine of all ♥♥♥ The Gift of Love.
♥ ♥ ♥ PETER HEERING

1

4

yes!

7

8–11 The theme of relative size is sometimes employed as a basis for symbolization, that is, designing a picture whose every detail speaks to a single thematic issue:

The Feminine Touch[6]

12–26 Women, more than men, are pictured using their fingers and hands to trace the outlines of an object or to cradle it or to caress its surface (the latter sometimes under the guise of guiding it), or to effect a "just barely touching" of the kind that might be significant between two electrically charged bodies. This ritualistic touching is to be distinguished from the utilitarian kind that grasps, manipulates, or holds:

8

What has happened to women has now happened to perfume

14

9

12

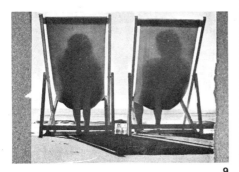

10

13

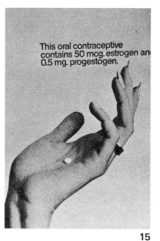

This oral contraceptive contains 50 mcg. estrogen and 0.5 mg. progestogen.

15

EQUAL PAY.
QUAL TIME.

BULOVA ACCUTRON

11

[6] Here and elsewhere in connection with the role of fingers (see pictures 295–320), I draw directly on observations made by Michi Ishida, to whom I give thanks.

This tiny bit of Moon Drops
Under Makeup Moisture Film

16

(continued)

ANDREA inv
WASH´N WE
Eyelas

introduc
Easy Care—Easy Wear E
the soakable droop-proof miracle lash that´s self-c
self-renewing, floating-light, virtually indestr
The most practical thing that´s happened to be
lashes to keep them beautiful since ANDREA mad

17

20

girl asleep on a guy's shoulder isn't so unusual. A girl asleep
The "Unbelievable"Wig by FashionTress

24

alcoolico al punto giust
profumato di natu
deciso e morbid
Jägermeiste
e per lui un magnific
aperitivo robust
per lei un ottim
digestivo gentil
per tutti semp
quel che ci vuo

Jägermeister

18

TRY SOMETHING BETTER

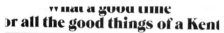

21

What a good time
or all the good things of a Kent

22

25

19

TISSOT

23

**Announcing new
Winston Light 100's**

Winston

Light   Extra length.
100's   Low tar.

26

27–8 Because nothing very prehensile is involved in these ritualistic touchings, the face can be used instead of a hand:

29–36 Self-touching can also be involved, readable as conveying a sense of one's body being a delicate and precious thing:

27

28

29

30

31

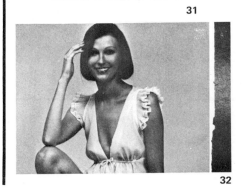

32

33

34

35

36

Function Ranking

In our society when a man and a woman collaborate face-to-face in an under- taking, the man—it would seem—is likely to perform the executive role, providing only that one can be fashioned. This arrangement seems widely represented in advertisements, in part, no doubt, to facilitate interpretability at a glance.

37–44   This hierarchy of functions is pictured within an occupational frame:[7]

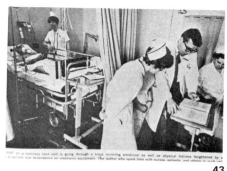

43

39

44

40

37

Sea Island-where else?

38

41

42

---

[7] The irony has been noted that an appre- ciable amount of the advertising aimed at selling supplies for women's household work employs males in the depicted role of instruct- ing professionals or employs a male celebrity to tout the efficacy of the product (see Komisar 1972:307).

45—58 It is also pictured outside of occupational specialization:

The Faces of Virginia

45

46

47

48

He's not a knight in shining armor.

49

50[8]

51

52

[8]Chalfen (1975:94) reports that in his American sample: "The male head of household used the camera most of the time. In a few cases, a teenage son, who was learning about cameras and filmmaking, took over this responsibility."

It happens every Salem.

53

54

Naturally!

Natural Menthol Blend

55

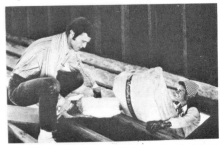

ReInsul can save you hundreds of dollars on fuel bills while keeping your home

56

(continued)

57

58

59–60 Function ranking is also pictured among children, albeit apparently with the understanding that although the little actors are themselves perfectly serious, their activity itself is not, being rather something that touchingly strikes an anticipatory note. In brief, "cuteness" is involved.[9]

59

60

61 All instruction seems to involve some sort of subordination of the instructed and deference for the instructor. These expressive features of the learning situation are reinforced by the linking of learning to age-grade subordination throughout most of the individual's learning career. In our society, one form of learning seems especially associated with child status, the "kinaesthetic" form,[10] involving a molding physical contact between instructor and instructed. Men seem to be pictured instructing women this way more than the reverse:

61

[9] A useful study of gender stereotypes in the illustrations of children's books is provided by Weitzman *et al.* (1972), for which I am methodologically grateful.

[10] The notion of kinaesthetic learning derives from Bateson and Mead (1942:85-86). This book brilliantly pioneered in the use of pictures for study of what can be neatly pictured. The work stimulated a whole generation of anthropologists to take pictures. However, very little analysis was—and perhaps could be—made of what these students collected. Somehow a confusion occurred between human interest and the analytical kind. Dandy movies and stills were brought home of wonderful people and fascinating events, but to little avail. Much respect and affection was shown the natives and little of either for the analytical use that can be made of pictures.

62–7 Whenever an adult receives body-addressed help or service from another, the resulting action is likely to involve collaboration of hands. The recipient guides the action and/or takes over at its terminal phases. (Examples: passing the salt or helping someone on with his coat.) In this way, presumably, the recipient's sense of autonomy is preserved. It is also preserved, of course, by his acquiring those skills through which he can efficiently tend to his own bodily needs. Infants and children, however, must suffer their hands being bypassed while an adult gets on with the job of looking after them.[11] It is understandable, then, that when adults are pictured in real scenes being spoon-fed, they are pictured guying the action in some way, presumably so the self projected by the act of being fed will not be taken as a reflection of the real one.

It appears that women are more commonly pictured receiving this kind of help from men than giving it to them, and are not depicted markedly guying their response:

Crème de Lindt.

66

63

64

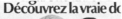

Découvrez la vraie do

65

Wilkins and the Lindsays: Surprise

62

67

---

[11] Admittedly there is the popular notion that members of the aristocratically inclined classes traditionally engaged personal servants to obtain body-connected care that members of the middle classes would want to provide for themselves, ashamedness here being a support of democracy. Of course, correlated with personal servicing was the non-person treatment of those who provided it.

68–71 Which raises the questions of how males are pictured when in the domains of the traditional authority and competence of females—the kitchen, the nursery, and the living room when it is being cleaned. One answer, borrowed from life and possibly underrepresented, is to picture the male engaged in no contributing role at all, in this way avoiding either subordination or contamination with a "female" task:

72–80 Another answer, I think, is to present the man as ludicrous or childlike, unrealistically so, as if perhaps in making him candidly unreal the competency image of real males could be preserved.

76

68

72

77

This is one of the best things made in America

69

73

78

70

74

79

71

75

80

81—3n   A subtler technique is to allow the male to pursue the alien activity under the direct appraising scrutiny of she who can do the deed properly, as though the doing were itself by way of being a lark or a dare, a smile on the face of the doer or the watcher attesting to the essentially unserious essayed character of the undertaking.[12]

81

82

[12] Correspondingly, when females are pictured engaged in a traditionally male task, a male may (as it were) parenthesize the activity, looking on appraisingly, condescendingly, or with wonder:

83n

The Family

The nuclear family as a basic unit of social organization is well adapted to the requirements of pictorial representation. All of the members of almost any actual family can be contained easily within the same close picture, and, properly positioned, a visual representation of the members can nicely serve as a symbolization of the family's social structure.

84

85—8   Turning to mocked-up families in advertisements, one finds that the allocation of at least one girl and at least one boy ensures that a symbolization of the full set of intrafamily relations can be effected. For example, devices are employed to exhibit the presumed special bond between the girl and the mother and the boy and the father, sometimes in the same picture:

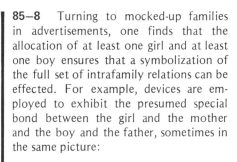

85

86

87

(continued)

88

89–99   Although in commercial scenes a unity is symbolized between fathers and sons and between mothers and daughters, there is a suggestion that different types of unity might be involved. In a word, there is a tendency for women to be pictured as more akin to their daughters (and to themselves in younger years) than is the case with men. Boys, as it were, have to push their way into manhood, and problematic effort is involved:

89

"Lights-Camera-Action"

90

Antonio y Cleopatra
the cigar that's going places

91

92

Girls merely have to unfold:

Can it be true?
Panties more comfortable than wearing nothing!

93

94

95

(continued)

96

97

98

99

100—14n Often the father (or in his absence, a son) stands a little outside the physical circle of the other members of the family, as if to express a relationship whose protectiveness is linked with, perhaps even requires, distance:

This Mother's Day, let your gift say it all.

100

"The sand...little flowers here and there... the sea and the sky. I love it."

101

102

103

104

105

106

107

(continued)

108 [13]

109

The Ritualization of Subordination

115–24   A classic stereotype of deference is that of lowering oneself physically in some form or other of prostration. Correspondingly, holding the body erect and the head high is stereotypically a mark of unashamedness, superiority, and disdain. Advertisers draw on (and endorse) the claimed universality of the theme:

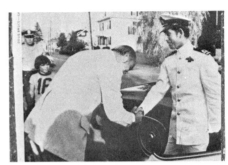

116

115

117

(continued)

---

[13] An interesting contrast is to be found in turn-of-the-century portrait poses of couples, wherein the effect was often achieved of displaying the man as the central figure and the woman as backup support, somewhat in the manner of a chief lieutenant. I cite from Lesy (1973):

110n

111n

112n

113n

114n

Perhaps the contrast between past and current portraits betokens a change less in underlying social organization than in conventions of expression within the picture format.

118

122

119

123

119

MRS. TONY JACKSON WITH THE BING CROSBYS
The women's glamor outfits by Werle and Jean Louis

120

124

121

125–39 Beds and floors provide places in social situations where incumbent persons will be lower than anyone sitting on a chair or standing. Floors also are associated with the less clean, less pure, less exalted parts of a room—for example, the place to keep dogs, baskets of soiled clothes, street footwear, and the like. And a recumbent position is one from which physical defense of oneself can least well be initiated and therefore one which renders one very dependent on the benignness of the surround. (Of course, lying on the floor or on a sofa or bed seems also to be a conventionalized expression of sexual availability.) The point here is that it appears that children and women are pictured on floors and beds more than are men.

125

126

127

(continued)

128

132

Some men are suited for games.
And some men are just better suited.

137

129

Marisa Berenson: Actress, model, aristocrat—and landed lovely of the Beautiful People

The Girl Who Has Everything Plus

133

138

Behind every great woman, there's a man.

134

130

135

139

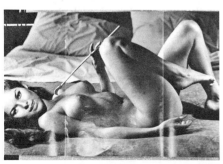

131

136

140–67   Although less so than in some, elevation seems to be employed indicatively in our society, high physical place symbolizing high social place. (Courtrooms provide an example.) In contrived scenes in advertisements, men tend to be located higher than women, thus allowing elevation to be exploited as a delineative resource.[14] A certain amount of contortion may be required. Note, this arrangement is supported by the understanding in our society that courtesy obliges men to favor women with first claim on whatever is available by way of a seat.

143

t fresh with Belair.
he right touch of menthol

147

140

144

When Greg saw his red Sherwin-Williams, he knew there was a Santa Claus

148

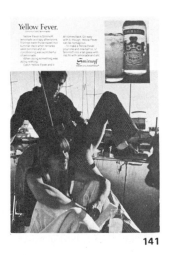

141

to lunch.

145

149

142

Votre "Première Rosières": une petite
es perfectionnements de cuisinières

146

To have
and to hold...
in sickness
and in health...

150

(continued)

---

[14] In such pictures as I have of actual scenes, the same tendency holds.

What to wear on Sunday
when you won't be home till Monday.

Happy Legs

151

155

158

152

156

159

153

154

Seagram's 7 Crown.
It fits right into your world.

157

160

161

(continued)

162

165

163

166

167

164

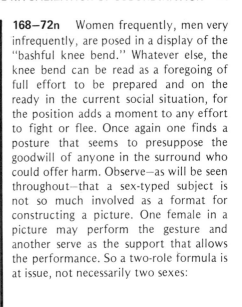

168

168–72n Women frequently, men very infrequently, are posed in a display of the "bashful knee bend." Whatever else, the knee bend can be read as a foregoing of full effort to be prepared and on the ready in the current social situation, for the position adds a moment to any effort to fight or flee. Once again one finds a posture that seems to presuppose the goodwill of anyone in the surround who could offer harm. Observe—as will be seen throughout—that a sex-typed subject is not so much involved as a format for constructing a picture. One female in a picture may perform the gesture and another serve as the support that allows the performance. So a two-role formula is at issue, not necessarily two sexes:

169

(continued)

170

176

173–86   Having somewhat the same distribution in ads as the knee bend are canting postures. Although a distinction can be made between body cant and head cant, the consequences seem to be much the same. The level of the head is lowered relative to that of others, including, indirectly, the viewer of the picture. The resulting configurations can be read as an acceptance of subordination, an expression of ingratiation, submissiveness, and appeasement.

173–8   Body cant:

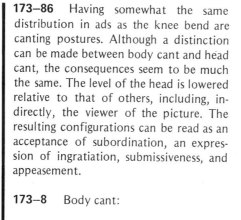

173[16]

171[15]

174

177

[15] Contrast a different kind of knee bend:

172n

175

178

[16] From Darwin (1872:53, fig. 6).

179—86   Head cant:

179

182

185

180

183

186

181

184

187–91 Smiles, it can be argued, often function as ritualistic mollifiers, signaling that nothing agonistic is intended or invited, that the meaning of the other's act has been understood and found acceptable, that, indeed, the other is approved and appreciated. Those who warily keep an eye on the movements of a potential aggressor may find themselves automatically smiling should their gaze be "caught" by its object, who in turn may find little cause to smile back. In addition, a responding smile (even more so an appreciative laugh) following very rapidly on the heels of a speaker's sally can imply that the respondent belongs, by knowledgeability, at least, to the speaker's circle. All of these smiles, then, seem more the offering of an inferior than a superior. In any case, it appears that in cross-sexed encounters in American society, women smile more, and more expansively, than men,[17] which arrangement appears to be carried over into advertisements, perhaps with little conscious intent.

189

DOCTORS TWO—Artist Andrew Wyeth of Chadds Ford has his academic robe adjusted by Nancy Hanks, chairman of the

187

"Bermuda has the limelight — and it has peace and tranquility."

188

190

191

192–206 Given the subordinated and indulged position of children in regard to adults, it would appear that to present oneself in puckish styling is to encourage the corresponding treatment. How much of this guise is found in real life is an open question; but found it is in advertisements.

LOVE AND HATE

Fig. 7. The "infant schema": the attributes of a small child (big head in relation to body, high prominent forehead, chubby cheeks, short rounded limbs, small mouth for sucking, etc.) are often greatly exaggerated in the dolls produced by the toy industry, which increases the protective-releasing effect of these "cute" little objects. In commercial art the childish attributes of women are frequently exag-

192

193

atch your woman a snowflak

194

[17]See the comments in Weisstein (1973:49).

(continued)

195

196

197

198

199

200

201

202

203

204

205

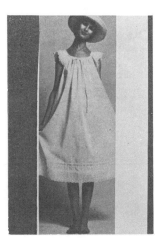

206

207–16 The note of unseriousness struck by a childlike guise is struck by another styling of the self, this one perhaps entirely restricted to advertisements, namely, the use of the entire body as a playful gesticulative device, a sort of body clowning:

210

214

207

211

215

208

212

209

213

216

217–23 The special unseriousness involved in childlike guises and clowning suggests a readiness to be present in a social situation garbed and styled in a manner to which one isn't deeply or irrevocably committed. Perhaps reflected here is a readiness to try out various guises and to appear at various times in different ones. In any case, in advertisements, at least, there seems to be an unanticipated difference between men and women. Men are displayed in formal, business, and informal gear, and although it seems understood that the same individual will at different times appear in all these guises, each guise seems to afford him something he is totally serious about, and deeply identified with, as though wearing a skin, not a costume. Even in the case of the cowboy garb that urban males affect recreationally, little sense that one's whole appearance is a lark would seem to be present. Women in ads seem to have a different relationship to their clothing and to the gestures worn with it. Within each broad category (formal, business, informal) there are choices which are considerably different one from another, and the sense is that one may as well try out various possibilities to see what comes of it—as though life were a series of costume balls. Thus, one can occasionally mock one's own appearance, for identification is not deep. It might be argued, then, that the costume-like character of female garb in advertisements locates women as less seriously present in social situations than men, the self presented through get-ups being itself in a way an unserious thing. Observe that the extension of this argument to real life need not involve a paradox. It is a common view that women spend much more of their time and concern in shopping for clothes and preparing for appearances than do men, and that women set considerable store on the appreciative or depreciative response they produce thereby. But, of course, so does an actor in a part he will never play again. A concern over carrying an appearance off does not necessarily imply a deep and abiding identification with that appearance. (This argument fits with the fact that women's styles change much more rapidly than do men's.)

217

218

219

220

221

222

223

224–43 Adults play mock assault games with children, games such as chase-and-capture and grab-and-squeeze. The child is playfully treated like a prey under attack by a predator. Certain materials (pillows, sprays of water, light beach balls) provide missiles that can strike but not hurt. Other materials provide a medium into which the captured body can be thrown safely—beds, snow banks, pools, arms. Now it turns out that men play these games with women, the latter collaborating through a display of attempts to escape and through cries of alarm, fear, and appeasement. (Figure-dancing provides occasion for an institutionalized example, the partners who are swung off their feet never being men.) Of course, underneath this show a man may be engaged in a deeper one, the suggestion of what he could do if he got serious about it. In part because mock assault is "fun" and more likely in holiday scenes than in work scenes, it is much represented in advertisements:

227

224

228

232

225

229

233

226

In love with
the little
mink jacket.

230

234

(continued)

"We were walking down b
when we saw these huge pa
They were just beautiful."

235

Salem refreshes natura

Naturally grown tobacco
Rich natural tobacco taste
No harsh, hot taste

Salem

239

The Outspoken

CHANEL

Witty. Confident. Devastatingly feminine.

CHANEL N°

243

crazy.

236

naturally!

240

Broil today's catch on the open
the Pipers Scotch. It's
moment. And you feel great.
girl. The whole mounts
And your very own Scotch. Rete
be smoother and neither could Piper
blended and bottled in
by Seagram: the world's foremost

Pipers: The Scotch to weekend w
any day of the

237

Refresh yours

Have a Salem,
smooth, rich tobaccos
refreshing menthol

Salem

241

After all, if
a pleasure,

ve with pleasure!   New

238

Wish you could take pictures like this?
Splash! Flash! You got it!

242

244–6 A male pictured with a female sometimes appears to employ an extended arm, in effect marking the boundary of his social property and guarding it against encroachment. A suggestion is that this miniature border patrol is especially found when the female at the same time is engaged in a pursuit which accords her authority.

247–69 There seem to be four main behavioral arrangements of pairs of persons which provide what is taken to be a physical expression that the two are a "with"—that is, together as a social unit with respect to the social situation in which they are located. (In all four cases, note, the work these dyadic tie-signs do in defining the relationship between figures in a picture would seem to be much the same as the work they do in real social situations.)

247–9 First, a matter of micro-ecology: sitting or standing close and alongside, with or without touching. This arrangement is symmetrical in physical character and social implication, no differentiation of role or rank being in itself conveyed:

250–3 The "arm lock" is the basic tie-sign in Western societies for marking that a woman is under the protective custody of the accompanying man. Although most commonly sustained between husband and wife, no sexual or legal link is necessarily advertised through it; father and grown daughter, man and best friend's wife may also employ it. The sign is asymmetric both in terms of its physical configuration and what it indicates. However nominally, the woman shows herself to be receiving support, and both the man's hands are free for whatever instrumental tasks may arise:

244

245

246

247

248

249

250

251

252

(continued)

Industries: the homemaking people?

253

254–60 The "shoulder hold" is an asymmetrical configuration more or less requiring that the person holding be taller than the person held, and that the held person accept direction and constraint. Typically the arrangement seems to be dyadically irreversible. When employed by a cross-sexed adult pair, the sign seems to be taken to indicate sexually-potential proprietaryship.

257

254

The Ellsbergs arrive at court: Was patriotism the issue?

TRIALS:
The Purloined Papers?

258

255

259

256

260

261–9 Finally, hand-holding. When employed between adult male and female, hand-holding appears to be taken to indicate a sexually potential, exclusive relationship.[18] A relatively symmetrical tie-sign presumably expressing relative equality. Physical asymmetry is to be detected in the tendency for the male to hold the female hand, this allowing the indication that he is presumably free to let go quickly should an emergency arise and free to guide and direct. The physical fact that the back of his hand is likely to be facing what is upcoming can faintly symbolize protectiveness:

The directing potential of hand-holding can be made apparent in ads:

263

267

261

264

So also another theme, that of the male providing a safe tether:

268

262

265

269

266

---

[18] Tie-signs in general and hand-holding in particular are considered in Goffman (1971: 188-237).

Licensed Withdrawal

Women more than men, it seems, are pictured engaged in involvements which remove them psychologically from the social situation at large, leaving them unoriented in it and to it, and presumably, therefore, dependent on the protectiveness and goodwill of others who are (or might come to be) present.

270—94 When emotional response causes an individual to lose control of his facial posture, that is, to "flood out", he can partly conceal the lapse by turning away from the others present or by covering his face, especially his mouth, with his hands. Ritualization of the kind associated with the young is involved, for the act cannot conceal that something is being concealed, and furthermore requires momentary blindness to everything around oneself—this being a particularly empty and maladaptive response when the withdrawal is itself a response to a real threat.

270—5 Remorse:

272

275

273

270

271

274

276—82   Fear:

276

280

283—8   Shyness:

277

281

278

282

283

284

285

279

286

(continued)

True Confessions
of an Olivetti girl.

(or, How a change
in typewriters
changed my life)

287

You've come a long wa

VIRGIN
SLIM

VIRGINI
SLIMS

288

289—94　Laughter:

EADY! AIM! TEE HEE!

289

290

sident Nixon laughing at a remark by Anatoly A. Dobrynin, the Soviet Ambassador,
ring a performance by the University of Minnesota Band in the White House Rose

291

Who's 30 and who's 22?
(Their hands won't tell)

292

293

294

295–309   Just as covering the mouth with the hand can be an attenuation of covering the face, so a finger brought to the mouth can be an attenuation of covering it with the hand. But here another ritualization seems more common: the attenuation of sucking or biting the finger. The impression is given that somehow a stream of anxiety, rumination, or whatever, has been split off from the main course of attention and is being sustained in a dissociated, unthinking fashion. In any case, the face is partly covered as though one could see but not be seen and were therefore free to engage hand and face outside the stream of face-to-face address:

298

302

299

303

295

304

300

296

305

297

301

(continued)

306

307

308

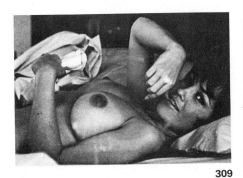

309

310–20 Finger-to-finger position appears to carry the same dissociated self-communication as is expressed in finger-to-mouth gestures but in a still more attenuated form. Displacement from mouth is a thinkable possibility.

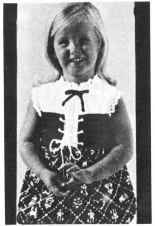

310

311

312

313

314

315

316

(continued)

317

320

321–2   Turning one's gaze away from another's can be seen as having the consequence of withdrawing from the current thrust of communication, allowing one's feelings to settle back into control while one is somewhat protected from direct scrutiny. Since flight is not exhibited in this gaze—aversive behavior, some sort of submission to and trust in the source of stimulus seems to be implied.[20]

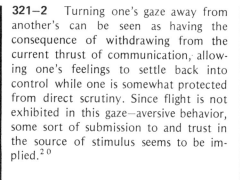

318[19]

321

319

322

[19] Note the combination of finger-to-finger with body cant and knee bend in this and the next two pictures.

[20] The process receives its canonical literary expression on a page in Joyce's *Portrait of an Artist as a Young Man*, here cited in full as a reminder that the novelistic sexism attributed to Mailer can run gently and deep:

A girl stood before him in midstream: alone and still, gazing out to sea. She seemed like one whom magic had changed into the likeness of a strange and beautiful seabird. Her long slender bare legs were delicate as a crane's and pure save where an emerald trail of seaweed had fashioned itself as a sign upon the flesh. Her thighs, fuller and softhued as ivory, were bared almost to the hips where the white fringes of her drawers were like feathering of soft white down. Her slate-blue skirts were kilted boldly about her waist and dovetailed behind her. Her bosom was as a bird's, soft and slight, slight and soft as the breast of some dark-plumaged dove. But her long fair hair was girlish: and girlish, and touched with the wonder of mortal beauty, her face.

She was alone and still, gazing out to sea; and when she felt his presence and the worship of his eyes her eyes turned to him in quiet suffrance of his gaze, without shame or wantonness. Long, long she suffered his gaze and then quietly withdrew her eyes from his and bent them towards the stream, gently stirring the water with her foot hither and thither. The first faint noise of gently moving water broke the silence, low and faint and whispering, faint as the bells of sleep; hither and thither, hither and thither: and a faint flame trembled on her cheek.

—Heavenly God! cried Stephen's soul, in an outburst of profane joy.—

The ethological source is Chance (1962).

323–38 Head/eye aversion. The lowering of the head presumably withdraws attention from the scene at hand, dependency entailed and indicated thereby. The gain is that one's feelings will be momentarily concealed—although, of course, not the fact that one is attempting such concealment. (As in head canting, height is reduced, contributing to a symbolization of submissiveness.) Mere aversion of the eyes can apparently serve similarly:

327

331

323

328

332

329

324

333

325

326

330

334

(continued)

335

336

337

338

339—47 In real social situations and in pictured ones, the individual can withdraw his gaze from the scene at large (with the dependency and trust that this implies) and lock it in such a way as to give the impression of having only minor dissociated concern with what is thus seen, even as his mind has wandered from everything in the situation; psychologically, he is "away." (Doodling and middle distance looks are examples, although it should be kept in mind that these two practices can also figure in another arrangement, the one in which the individual aurally attends to what is being said by another while making it apparent that nothing he can see is competing for attention.)

339

340

341

342

343

344

(continued)

An interesting object on which to lock an away look is the hands, for this focus not only can convey some sort of self-enclosure, but also can require a downward turning of the head, submissiveness being a possible consequent interpretation:

348—72 In advertisements women are shown mentally drifting from the physical scene around them (that is, going "away") while in close physical touch with a male, as though his aliveness to the surround and his readiness to cope with anything that might present itself were enough for both of them. (At the same time, the male may well wear a wary, monitoring look.) Thus, "anchored drifts". Various points of visual focus are found.

348—61 Middle distance:

351

345

348

352

346

349

353

347

350

354

(continued)

355

356

357

358

359

id a milder moment   360

361

362–7   Small objects:

362

363

364

(continued)

365

366

367 (see also 335)

368–72 A twistable part of the male's clothing:

368

369

370

371

372

373–5 Maintaining a telephone conversation necessarily means some withdrawal of attention from the immediate scene at hand, with attendant lack of orientation to, and readiness for, events that might occur therein. This can be controlled by limiting the length of calls and one's involvement in what is talked about. In advertisements women are sometimes shown luxuriating in a call, immersing themselves in a dreamy and presumably prolonged way.

373

374

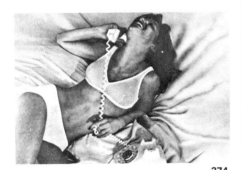

375

376–8 In advertisements, women are not only posed lying on the floor or in a bed, but also at the same time bending their legs as though that part of the body were being employed in a dissociated way, as in doodling, except here the dissociated behavior is large scale, as might therefore be the attention it withdraws from the scene at large:

376

377

378

379–95 It has already been remarked that in ads women, more than men, appear to withdraw themselves from the social situation at hand through involvements, including emotional response. Significant here are the responses of pleasure, delight, laughter, and glee—states of being transported by happiness. Perhaps the implication is that a woman—like a child with an ice cream cone—can find some sort of final satisfaction in goals that can be fully realized in the present.[21] In consequence, a consumatory "flooding out":

379

(continued)

[21] A similar argument is suggested by Komisar (1972:306-307):

If television commercials are to be believed, most American women go into uncontrollable ecstasies at the sight and smell of tables and cabinets that have been lovingly caressed with long-lasting, satin-finish, lemon-scented, spray-on furniture polish. Or they glow with rapture at the blinding whiteness of their wash—and the green-eyed envy of their neighbors. The housewife in the Johnson's Wax commercial hugs the dining room table because the shine is so wonderful; then she polishes herself into a corner and has to jump over the furniture to get out. Bold detergent shows one woman in deep depression because her wash is not as bright as her neighbor's.

Observe that in advertisements, instead of our being shown a woman's flood of pleasure upon receipt of a present from a man, we may be shown the scene that might have just preceded that one, namely, the "Guess what?" scene, wherein the man holds something beyond the vision of the woman (sometimes by obliging her to cover her eyes) and teasingly invites her to guess what her life is about to be enriched by, the prospect of which is seen to throw her into a state of joyous torment. Another version has the giver spring the surprise without warning, in consequence of which the recipient momentarily loses all self-control, breaking into a flutter of pleasure. These teasing uses of indulgence are, of course, commonly employed by parents in connection with their children, and are to be considered alongside another playful threat to equilibrium, one already touched on, namely, mock assault.

A corollary is that when a male and female are pictured in a euphoric state, the female is likely to be exhibiting a more expansive expression than is the male, which in turn fits with the argument already made and illustrated that in our society women smile more than men—both in real scenes and in commercially contrived ones:

380

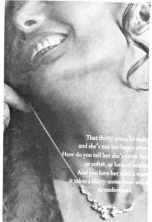

381

382

383

384

385

386

387

HARPER

388

389

390

(continued)

391

392

393

394

395

396—437 It is possible to look in on a social situation from a distance or from behind a one-way panel—a "participation shield"—and be little seen oneself, in which case one can, in effect, partake of the events but not be exposed to scrutiny or address. A splitting up thus results between some of the gains and some of the costs of face-to-face interaction. I might note that when one's participation is thus shielded, simultaneous maintenance of dissociated side involvements would seem to be facilitated, since these could hardly intrude between oneself and one's availability to the others in the situation—one not being available at all.

396

A ritualization of participation shielding occurs when one presents oneself as if on the edge of the situation or otherwise shielded from it physically, when in fact one is quite accessible to those in it. Still further ritualization is found in commercial posings.

397—400n   At the edge:

Love's A Little Cover is a sheer, smooth makeup
that covers so well, you'll look fresh and soft even in daylig

397

398

399[22]

_____

[22]Contrast this picture of hedged participation with one that is formally similar but
suggesting no protective participation:

400n

401—5   From behind objects:

Johnnie
Walker
Red

401

402

The Parliament recessed filter.
works like a cigarette holder works.

403

Princess Gard
leather accessories i
beautiful places to t
all the blah details i
Like credit ca
keys, combs, white
All our access
incredibly slim. De
spacious. Obvious!
All in all, a fal
to get rid of your cl
adding to your styl

404

WOW!
FAMOUS NAME
SEPARATES AT
15.99

GIMBELS

405

406—8   From behind animals:

406

407

408

409—37   From behind a person (with the consequent opportunity to overlay distance with a differentiating expression, in the extreme, collusive betrayal of one's shield):

The past is only a beginning

409

410

Sophie Baker
Diana Rigg and Menachem Gueffen

411

Mark Spitz and wife Suzy
Newsweek

412

MOVIES

NOX BL

Song and Dance Man

413

414

415

(continued)

So smooth, it's the fastest-growing
Light Whiskey in America.

416

420

ROYAL SYST

424

417

421

425

418

422

426

419

423

Sure you could get a perfectly good

427

(continued)

428

429

430

431

432

433

434

435[23]

436

437

[23] It should not be assumed that mere physical placement is involved here. Men are routinely pictured in a rear position in a manner implying anything but coyness and dependence (see, for example, pictures 100—14n and 244—6). As typical in these matters, the same verbal description of relative "physical" position could be equally applied to cover radically different effects. For the effective reading of his text, the writer depends upon effective viewing by his readers—words here serving to point, not specify.

438—78 Snuggling: among primates the very young turn, or are turned, into their mothers' bodies for comfort and protection, sometimes further cut off from the surrounding situation by enclosure within her arms. Perhaps the suckling position is the prototype, although for a child any adult in a parental role seems qualified as something to snuggle into.[24] As the child grows up, the insulation this practice objectively provides from the surrounding scene decreases progressively; eventually the withdrawal achieved this way can only be ritualistic. Whatever the biological roots of this snuggling practice, it is a resource in the formulating of commercial pictures.

438—44 Children:

440

444

438

441

442

439

443

---

[24] An ethological position on these postures is presented in Eibl-Eibesfeldt (1972:120-124). I am very grateful to Professor Eibl-Eibesfeldt for permission to reprint three pictures (192, 283 and 284) from *Love and Hate*.

445–8   Adults, lying:

The Hasanlu lovers

445

446

447

448

449–62   Sitting:

lecting the wave of American cultural change,

449

450

451

He uses
the same line
on everyone.

452

453

454

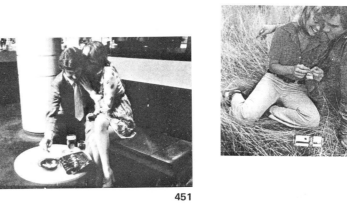

455

456

(continued)

457

458

459

460

461

462

463–8   One sitting, one standing:

463

464

Wool. It's got life.

465

(continued)

466

467

468

469–78   Standing:

469

470

471

472

473

474

475

(continued)

476

477

478

479—86 Nuzzling—apparently an attenuated form of snuggling—involves employment of the face and especially the nose as a sort of surrogate or substitute for tucking in the whole body. Nuzzling, then, would seem to constitute a form of partial withdrawal from full availability to the situation at large. What one finds, in pictures at least, is that women nuzzle children but men apparently do not. Indeed, women are sometimes pictured nuzzling objects. And, of course, women are pictured nuzzling men.

479

480

481

482

483

484

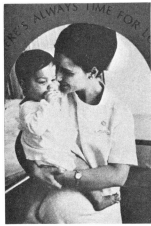

485

(continued)

The Lambert Look in gold and diamond jewelry is young and fresh, contemporary—and timeless, bridal sets like these, in 18 karat sculptured yellow gold. Top: Diamond solitaire.

486

487–96 The process whereby an individual snuggles into another seems anything but impersonal, and yet is (I feel) related to something that has an impersonal cast, namely, the use of another's body as if it were something that could be used at will, without apparent reference to its possessor, as an object to lean on or rest one's limbs on, in short, as a physical resource, not a socially responsive one. In many cases, note, such leaning use of another seems to be an attenuated, very ritualized, form of snuggling. Note also that a non-sexual implication is present in the contact, and that, in advertisements at least, women (much as do children with respect to adults) apparently have license to use more of a man's body in this utilitarian way than the reverse. The assumption seems to be that a woman is less likely to have sexual intent than a man, and that her use of his body is therefore less suspect than his of hers. (Of course, an added factor is the understanding that he will be able to bear her weight much more easily than she his.) Note, the configurations here considered involve individuals in a personal relationship, typically a sexually potential one. Among the less close, the license to touch follows a different pattern. Men can punctuate their verbal interaction with women by showing support, protectiveness, good will, and parent-like affection, through the laying on of the hand, a license apparently less available to women (and other subordinates) in their dealings with men (see Henley 1973).

487

The boy by Mrs. Gavin.
The boy's shirt by Kaynee.

488

489

490

(continued)

491

494

It's coming-out time for you

492

495

497–500 A very standardized two-person asymmetrical configuration observable in real life and often in pictures is the "grief embrace." All combinations of sex are found in the two roles, except, apparently, that women are not pictured providing this sort of comfort to men.[25] Whether in life or in pictures, one is provided here with a nice example of formalization—the reduction of multiple configurations to a rather set ritualistic manoeuvre:

497

498

(continued)

493

Newport

496

[25] This distribution is not, I think, the basic one in our society. For there are many ritual practices of a supportive, bonding kind that women can extend to women or men, that men can extend to women, but that men can't extend to men. Kissing and terms of endearment such as "honey", "dear", "love" are examples. Indeed, a wide range of supportive practices may have a common, natural social history, beginning as something adults extend to children and then moving on through the following sequence of accretions: women-to-women, women-to-men, men-to-women, men-to-men.

499

501–8 The grief embrace appears to manifest itself in an attenuated, hyper-ritualized form, namely, arm support given as evidence of some sort of commendation or moral approval. Again, in commercial pictures, women do not seem to be shown giving this support to men.

ME SCHREIBER, a graduate of Purdue, and a Volunteer in Tanganyika.

504

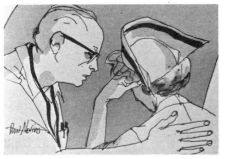

500

501

But you've told him plenty.

On the subject of drinking, it's not only what you say,
it's how you act.

505

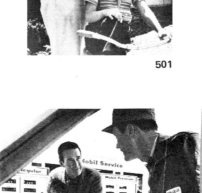

502

506

503

507

(continued)

id you know that
the Queen of England
wanted bone china
r her wedding table,
e chose Aynsley?

Oh, yes, dear,
d when the president's
ughter wanted crystal,
he chose Waterford.

508

Conclusion

Under display have been "natural" expressions of gender insofar as these can be represented in commercial advertising through visually accessible behavioral style. I believe that upon examination these expressions turn out to be illustrations of ritual-like bits of behavior which portray an ideal conception of the two sexes and their structural relationship to each other, accomplishing this in part by indicating, again ideally, the alignment of the actor in the social situation.

Commercial photographs, of course, involve carefully performed poses presented in the style of being "only natural." But it is argued that actual gender expressions are artful poses, too.

From the perspective of ritual, then, what is the difference between the scenes depicted in advertisements and scenes from actual life? One answer might be "hyper-ritualization." The standardization, exaggeration, and simplification that characterize rituals in general are in commercial posings found to an extended degree, often rekeyed as babyishness, mockery, and other forms of unseriousness. Another answer is found in the process of editing. A commercial photograph is a ritualization of social ideals with all the occasions and senses in which the ideal is not exhibited having been cut away, edited out of what is made available. In ordinary life we conspire to provide the same kind of "natural" expressions, but we can only do this by means of behavioral style or at particular junctures in our course of activity—moments of ceremony, occasions for giving sympathy, sudden access to friends, and similar junctures in the daily round, as determined by a schedule we know little about as yet. So both in advertisements and life we are interested in colorful poses, in externalization; but in life we are, in addition, stuck with a considerable amount of dull footage. Nonetheless, whether we pose for a picture or execute an actual ritual action, what we are presenting is a commercial, an ideal representation under the auspices of its characterizing the way things really are. When a man in real life lights a cigarette for a woman, the presupposition is that females are worthy objects, physically limited in some way, and that they should be helped out in all their transitions. But this "natural" expression of the relation between the sexes, this little interpersonal ritual, may be no more an actual reflection of the relationship between the sexes than is the couple pictured in the cigarette ad a representative couple. Natural expressions are commercials performed to sell a version of the world under conditions no less questionable and treacherous than the ones that advertisers face.

By and large, advertisers do not create the ritualized expressions they employ; they seem to draw upon the same corpus of displays, the same ritual idiom, that is the resource of all of us who participate in social situations, and to the same end: the rendering of glimpsed action readable. If anything, advertisers conventionalize our conventions, stylize what is already a stylization, make frivolous use of what is already something considerably cut off from contextual controls. Their hype is hyper-ritualization.

REFERENCES CITED

Bateson, Gregory, and Margaret Mead
  1942 The Balinese Character. New York: New York Academy of Science.
Chalfen, Richard
  1975 Cinéma Naiveté: A Study of Home Moviemaking as Visual Communication. Studies in the Anthropology of Visual Communication 2:87-103.
Chance, M. R. A.
  1962 An Interpretation of Some Agonistic Postures: The Role of "Cut-Off" Acts and Postures. Symposium of the Zoological Society of London 8:71-89.
Darwin, Charles
  1872 On the Expression of the Emotions in Man and Animals. London: John Murray.
Eibl-Eibesfeldt, Irenäus
  1972 Love and Hate. Geoffrey Strachan, trans. New York: Holt, Rinehart and Winston.
Goffman, Erving
  1971 Relations in Public. New York: Basic Books.
  1974 Frame Analysis. New York: Harper and Row.
Henley, Nancy
  1973 The Politics of Touch. In Radical Psychology. Phil Brown, ed. Pp. 421-433. New York: Harper and Row.
Komisar, Lucy
  1972 The Image of Woman in Advertising. In Woman in Sexist Society. Vivian Gornick and Barbara K. Moran, eds. New York: New American Library.
Lesy, Michael
  1973 Wisconsin Death Trip. New York: Pantheon.
Robinson, Dwight E.
  1976 Fashions in Shaving and Trimming of the Beard: The Men of the Illustrated London News, 1842-1972. American Journal of Sociology 81(5):1131-1141.
Sudnow, David
  1972 Temporal Parameters of Interpersonal Observation. In Studies in Social Interaction. David Sudnow, ed. Pp. 259-279. New York: The Free Press.
Weisstein, Naomi
  1973 Why We Aren't Laughing Any More. MS 2:49-90.
Weitzman, Lenore J., Deborah Eifler, Elizabeth Hokada, and Catherine Ross
  1972 Sex-Role Socialization in Picture Books for Preschool Children. American Journal of Sociology 77(6): 1125-1150.